Breakfast

BAKES

Breakfast BAKES

SWEET AND SAVOURY RECIPES FOR GOOD MORNINGS

Elizabeth Wolf-Cohen

APPLE

A QUINTET BOOK

Published by the Apple Press
6 Blundell Street
London N7 9BH

ISBN 1-85076-830-7

This book was designed and produced by
Quintet Publishing Limited
6 Blundell Street
London N7 9BH

creative director: RICHARD DEWING
art director: CLARE REYNOLDS
design: BALLEY DESIGN ASSOCIATES
designers: SIMON BALLEY AND JOANNA HILL
project editor: DOREEN PALAMARTSCHUK
editor: JANE HURD-COSGRAVE
photographer: AMANDA HEYWOOD

Typeset in Great Britain by
Central Southern Typesetters, Eastbourne
Manufactured in Singapore by United Graphic Pte Ltd
Printed in China by Leefung-Asco Pte Ltd

contents

INTRODUCTION

Breakfast Bakes is a collection of recipes for home-baked goods—that will help you start the day with a smile. What could be more appealing than the aroma of fresh Warm Orange Muffins on a cold winter morning, or an elegant Almond Croissant with an espresso coffee for a lazy Sunday brunch time? This collection is a combination of easy quick breads and slightly more complicated yeast breads, which can be served for family breakfasts, coffee mornings with friends, brunches, afternoon teas or snacks—even as desserts. In fact, they are delicious any time.

Muffins, quick breads, tea breads and scones fall into the category of quick breads, that is, baked goods using baking powder or bicarbonate of soda, or even just beaten eggs as a raising agent. They are quick to assemble and bake. Yeast breads, such as brioche, savoury loaves or Danish-style cakes and buns, are risen by both the action of yeast and the process of kneading and rising.

Ingredients

Most quick breads are combinations of types of flour, fat, sweetener, a rising agent and flavourings; some contain eggs, but some don't. Yeast breads, of course, contain yeast.

FLOUR is the main ingredient in breads; it is the gluten in flour that gives bread and baked goods their structure. White and wholemeal flours can be used separately or combined to produce various textures. Other flours and grains, such as corn, oat, rye, soya, cornmeal, oatmeal, wheat grain, bran and rice can add variety and texture. Most of the recipes in this book call for plain flour. If a mixture or dough looks dry or crumbly, add a little more of the liquid, water or milk to achieve a well blended mixture. As wholemeal and rye flours produce a very heavy result, it is best to mix them with plain flour, but remember that flour can vary, depending on the level of humidity and how long it has been stored, so the amount necessary may vary.

FATS such as butter, margarine, oil, lard and suet add flavour, moistness and colour to breads. I prefer a light-textured oil, such as sunflower, to the heavier corn oils for making muffins and quick breads. Avoid blended vegetable oils, as the blend may not be known, and also may not give good results. I generally prefer to bake with unsalted butter because it usually has a lower moisture content, and the amount of salt in the recipe can be more easily controlled. Remember to soften the butter to room temperature, unless a recipe stipulates chilled or cold butter. *Soften hard butter or margarine in a microwave-safe dish on full power for 5-second intervals until it is soft, but be careful not to let it melt.*

LIQUIDS Many muffins and quick breads use a combination of eggs and a liquid such as milk, water, fruit juices, buttermilk, soured cream or yogurt to help bind the mixture. The liquid used depends very much on the other ingredients and their flavours, as well as the desired texture. Buttermilk is one of my favourites, as it gives a moist, tender crumb to almost any cake or bread. Unless you are an experienced baker, do not substitute one liquid for another unless a recipe indicates, as other ingredients, such as rising agents, may then need to be altered as well.

EGGS help to bind breads, as well as adding flavour, texture and protein. Be sure to use eggs at room temperature, since adding cold eggs to a creamed butter mixture or a yeast sponge can cause curdling, and may reduce the action of the yeast. All the eggs used in these recipes are large.

Fresh honeycomb

SWEETENERS ranging from sugar to honey or maple syrup or molasses, add lots of flavour and moisture to different breads. Sweeteners bring out the flavours and small amounts of sugar are often added to savoury muffins, scones or quick breads for that reason. Liquid sweeteners, like honey or molasses, improve the keeping quality of baked goods, as well as increasing their moisture.

RAISING AGENTS Quick breads (muffins, scones, tea breads, pancakes and waffles) use *chemical raising agents* to raise a mixture. When mixed with liquids, baking powder and bicarbonate of soda create carbon dioxide bubbles in the mixture that raise the mixture when it is heated. Baking powder is used in many recipes. Mixtures containing baking powder must be mixed quickly, and then baked immediately. Bicarbonate of soda is often used in combination with other acid ingredients, such as buttermilk, soured cream, yogurt, lemon juice, honey or molasses. Store chemically-made raising agents in a cool, dark place, replace bicarbonate of soda every 3 to 4 months.

YEAST is the raising agent used to make most breads, and also in many sweet yeast doughs used for yeast cakes and sweet yeast breads. Yeast is available in three forms: fresh yeast, dried yeast and easy-blend yeast. The recipes in this book use dried yeast, since it is more easily available. 'Proving' the yeast is the first step in the recipes in this book. The yeast is dissolved in water with a little sugar before adding the dry ingredients. This ensures the yeast is active and begins the initial fermentation. Yeast is best dissolved in water, about 2 to 3 tablespoons per 7 g/¼ oz packet and left to foam and

Fresh yeast

froth. If it does not froth at all after 10 to 15 minutes, discard it and start again. Easy-blend yeast does not require this process, and is mixed directly with the dry ingredients. Some require only one rising, while others require two—it is important to read the instructions carefully.

KNEADING distributes the yeast throughout the dough and activates the gluten, which becomes elastic and expands when baked, giving texture and structure to breads. To knead the dough, turn it onto a lightly floured surface; using the heel of your hand, fold the dough and push down away from yourself, curving your fingers over the dough. Turn, fold, then push down and away again; repeat until the dough is smooth and elastic, and you can see small bubbles under the surface. The dough then needs to be left in a warm place to rise. A draught-free area of about 25–30°C/80–85°F is ideal. When the dough is about doubled in volume, check by pressing a fingertip into the dough. If the indentation remains, the dough has doubled and can be 'knocked back'. Push your fist into the centre of the dough to deflate it, then place on a lightly floured surface and knead a few times.

Cinnamon sticks and nutmeg

FLAVOURINGS of different kinds can produce a variety of taste sensations. Choose real essences such as vanilla, almond or rum to add a wonderful aroma and to accentuate the other flavours. Spices such as ground cinnamon, ginger and cloves give a warm spicy feel. Try to use freshly grated nutmeg in all your baked goods, as the difference is incomparable. Herbs, seeds, fruits and vegetables can also be used to add flavours. Be sure to toast nuts lightly before adding to mixtures, as this really helps to bring out their flavour.

EQUIPMENT

Most of the recipes in this book can be produced with the basic baking utensils found in the average kitchen. If you like muffins, it is worth investing in the newer, nonstick bakeware on the market as only minimal greasing is required. I prefer to use a vegetable cooking spray, as it is quick and easy. Alternatively, use a pastry brush to butter or grease the bakeware. Paper and foil cases also eliminate fussy clean-up, and using various colours and designs will make pretty 'packaging'.

Most tea breads are baked in 23 x 13 x 7.5-cm/9 x 5 x 3-inch or 20 x 10 x 6.5-cm/8 x 4 x 2½-inch loaf tins. Again, nonstick tins are always a good choice.

Methods

Quick breads are quick and easy to prepare, and while yeast breads require extra time for proving and kneading, many of the same baking principles apply.

Always **preheat the oven** as indicated. Most baked goods and breads require a quick blast of heat at the start of the rising action; the temperature can be reduced for recipes that require longer baking times. For even results, bake on the middle oven shelf. Prepare any bakeware as directed before you start so the mixture or dough can be baked immediately, then assemble all the ingredients and prepare any that need it beforehand.

As with all baking, **accurate measuring is essential**. Make sure your scales are measuring accurately. For baking powder,

bicarbonate of soda, salt and spices, use tablespoon and teaspoon measures, not a spoon from your kitchen drawer. Use a clean measuring jug for liquids, and check the amount at eye level for accuracy.

Combining the ingredients for all baked goods is very important, as it determines the texture of the end result. Muffins and quick breads should be mixed lightly only until the flour is just incorporated. Although the consistency of different mixtures might vary, the texture should be slightly lumpy. If over-mixed until completely smooth, the texture will be slightly dry and tough. Scones should never be over-mixed or over-kneaded, as they will be dense and tough-textured. Mix the dough until it just holds together, then knead lightly until the dough is well combined, but not smooth and elastic. On the other hand, yeast breads need complete and thorough mixing and kneading to distribute the yeast evenly throughout the dough, and need to be re-kneaded well to activate the gluten.

Mixture should be **spooned lightly** into muffin-tin cups and loaf tins; let the mixture drop gently from the spoon, or scoop it into the cups or tin, and remember not to pat down or smooth the tops of the muffins. Try to spoon quick bread mixtures evenly into tins so the tops do not require much handling. Yeast doughs are generally more resilient, although care should be taken not to stretch dough when arranging on, or transferring, to baking sheets. Most baking should be done in single layers on the middle oven shelf, as this allows for the

air to circulate evenly. Baking times are a guide; it is a good idea to begin checking to see if it is done after the minimum time.

Doneness can be judged in many ways; usually the baked goods will smell, and will have just begun to shrink from the side of the tin. For plain mixtures, a fine skewer or wooden cocktail stick inserted into the centre of the muffin, loaf or cake will come out clean. Other mixtures may have ingredients that will contain moisture or solid ingredients such as dried or chopped, fresh fruits or vegetables, which make testing more difficult. These are best tested by pressing with a fingertip. If the surface springs back lightly, it should be done; however, it is preferable to underbake slightly than overbake, and baked goods will generally continue to cook for a few minutes after being removed from the oven. A good test for yeast breads is to invert them out of the tin and onto a rack, and then tap the bottom with your knuckles; the bread should sound hollow. Rolls and coffee cakes are usually fully done when risen and golden.

Most muffins, quick breads and yeast breads can be unmoulded or removed from the tin very quickly after baking. Muffins and quick breads will become damp and soggy if left in their tin too long. Muffins can be removed immediately, although leaving them to cool for about two minutes will ensure that they are set. Quick breads should be left for a few minutes before turning out. Because yeast breads are more solid, they can be turned out or slid onto a wire rack straight away. Some coffee cakes can be treated like quick breads, but because many have toppings, they are best cooled in their tins, or as directed, before careful unmoulding.

Muffins and scones are **best when eaten immediately** or on the same day. Most quick breads benefit from complete cooling and storing overnight; this helps to develop their flavour, and makes for easier slicing. Before storing, cool all baked goods, then wrap them in cling film or foil. To freeze, place in freezer bags, label and store in freezer. To thaw, transfer to the refrigerator for several hours before serving, or thaw for 2 to 3 hours at room temperature. For really quick, 'freezer-to-table' muffins, line a muffin tin with paper or foil cases. Fill with the mixture and freeze immediately. When frozen, remove the filled cups to a plastic freezer bag or container, label them, and mark the baking time and temperature. When ready to

bake, just drop the frozen muffins into the tin and bake, adding about five minutes to the baking time.

Hot tips for muffins, scones, and quick breads

Remember the following tips to help you make successful muffins, scones, biscuits, and quick breads every time:

- **Do not overmix**—This tip cannot be overemphasized. If you stir until the batter is smooth, you will get a tough, dry result with tunnels or holes. Stir wet and dry ingredients together just until combined; the batter **should** be slightly lumpy.
- Unless specified, have all your ingredients ready and at room temperature before you start, especially butter and eggs.
- Shiny baking pans reflect heat, while dark, dull pans absorb it. If using a dark, nonstick pan, first reduce the heat by 25°F, and then put a bowl of water on the bottom of the oven for moisture. Bake all cakes and breads in a single layer on the middle oven-shelf or rack.
- For an evenly rounded muffin top, only grease the bottom and ½ inch up the side of the cup.
- Bake muffins and quick breads as soon as they are mixed, since both baking powder and soda begin their raising action as soon as they are moistened.
- To avoid soggy sides and bottoms, remove the muffins from the pan almost immediately after removing them from the oven. Cool quick breads for slightly longer.
- Begin checking for doneness after the minimum baking time indicated.
- Day-old muffins, scones, and biscuits can be split and toasted, then served with butter or preserves for a delicious breakfast treat.
- For "instant muffins," mix the dry ingredients and wet ingredients separately (wet ingredients should not be mixed more than 2 to 3 hours ahead) and grease the pan. When ready, preheat the oven, mix, and bake.

- Never over-knead biscuit or scone dough. Lightly folding and pressing between 8 to 12 times is enough to distribute the ingredients evenly.
- For soft-sided biscuits, bake close together. Arrange the shapes at least 2 inches apart for a crisper, crustier finish.

Handy hints for coffeecake and yeast breads

- Use a thermometer to check liquids before adding yeast; choose a warm place for raising dough.
- Check bread for doneness by tapping the bottom of the loaf with your knuckles; it should sound hollow.
- Dough textures vary, and can range from soft and slightly sticky to firm, smooth doughs. Doughs for firm, chewy bread should be very firm, while medium-firm doughs are fine for savory breads. Most coffee cake and sweet-yeast bread doughs are soft and some can even be quite sticky.
- For kneading, fold the dough, then push down and away from you with the heel of your hand, slightly curving your fingers over the edge. Turn the dough and repeat.
- For raising the dough, place in an oiled bowl, and turn to coat the dough with oil; this prevents a crust from forming over the surface. Alternatively, slide the dough in its bowl into a large, plastic bag, and seal tightly, allowing room for expansion.
- To check if the dough has doubled in volume, press a finger into the dough. If the hole remains, the dough is ready to be punched down.
- To punch down the dough, push your fist into the center of the dough, pulling the edges to the center, knead once or twice. Alternatively, turn the dough onto a lightly floured surface; it will automatically deflate. Knead once or twice.

FLAVOURED BUTTERS AND SPREADS

Easy-to-make, flavoured butters and spreads are a great way to make extra-special baked goods. They can be used to enhance or complement flavours, or served with simple muffins, quick breads or other baked goods to make them more unique. Savoury butters and cream cheese spreads can bring out the flavour of an ordinary bread.

Basic Sweet Butter

makes about 175 g/6 oz

115 g/4 oz butter (unsalted or salted), softened

2 to 3 tbsp sugar (or to taste)

2 tsp grated lemon or orange rind

Beat the butter, sugar and lemon or orange rind until soft, creamy and well blended. Scrape into a bowl and refrigerate, covered, until ready to serve. Soften at room temperature for at least 10 minutes for easier spreading.

Sweet Date Butter

makes about 400 g/14 oz

225 g/8 oz unsalted butter, softened

175 g/6 oz chopped stoned dates

1 to 2 tbsp honey

½ tsp ground cardamom or cinnamon

Put all the ingredients in the bowl of a food processor, fitted with the metal blade (be sure there are no odd date stones floating about!). Process until smooth and creamy, scraping down the side of the bowl once or twice. Scrape into a bowl and refrigerate, covered, until ready to serve.

VARIATIONS

ORANGE BUTTER Add an extra teaspoon of grated orange rind and 1 tablespoon of orange juice to the basic sweet butter.

FRUIT BUTTERS Add 2 to 3 tablespoons or more of mashed fruit, fruit purée or fruit jam, such as raspberry, strawberry, mango, banana, peach, nectarine, blackberry or pear to the basic sweet butter recipe. Add a pinch of cinnamon, nutmeg or ginger, depending on the fruit and your personal taste. Stir well together and refrigerate for later use.

Other flavoured butter variations are included with individual recipes in this book.

Sweet Cream Cheese Spread

makes about 225 g/8 oz

225 g/8 oz cream cheese, softened

2 tbsp brown sugar or honey

Beat the cream cheese together with the sugar or honey until soft and creamy and well blended, then add any of the following:

2 tbsp grated orange or lemon rind

75 g/3 oz orange, lemon or ginger marmalade

25 g/1 oz nuts, chopped

40 g/1½ oz raisins

VARIATIONS

TROPICAL FRUIT SPREAD To basic, sweet cream cheese spread, add: 40 g/1½ oz drained, crushed pineapple, 25 g/1 oz desiccated coconut, ½ teaspoon freshly grated nutmeg or ground ginger and ½ teaspoon rum essence.

Maple Walnut Butter

makes 175 g/6 oz

115 g/4 oz butter, softened to room temperature

1 tbsp maple syrup

40 g/1½ oz toasted walnuts, finely chopped

In a medium bowl with an electric mixer, beat the softened butter until light and creamy. Beat in the maple syrup, then stir in the walnuts until blended. Spoon into a bowl and refrigerate, covered, until ready to serve.

Brown Sugar and Cream Cheese Spread

makes about 250 g/9 oz

225 g/8 oz cream cheese, softened

1 tbsp honey

2 to 3 tbsp caster sugar or light brown sugar

½ tsp ground cinnamon

2 tbsp walnuts, finely chopped (optional)

Beat the cream cheese with the honey, sugar and cinnamon in a medium bowl. If you like, stir in 2 tablespoons of finely chopped walnuts. Store as for the sweet butters.

Herby Butter or Cream Cheese Spread

makes about 225 g/8 oz

225 g/8 oz butter or cream cheese, softened

Salt and freshly ground black pepper, to taste

1 small clove garlic, crushed (optional)

2 tbsp chopped fresh herbs, such as parsley, dill, thyme, tarragon, oregano or chives, or use dried mixed herbs.

Beat the ingredients together until smooth and creamy. Store as for the sweet butters.

Parmesan Butter

makes about 225 g/8 oz

225 g/8 oz butter, softened

Salt and freshly ground black pepper, to taste

1 small clove garlic, crushed

3 tbsp freshly grated Parmesan cheese

¼ tsp dried basil or oregano

1 to 2 tbsp chopped fresh chives or parsley

Beat the ingredients together until soft and well blended. Store as for other butters.

Herby Spring Onion Cream Cheese Spread

makes about 225 g/8 oz

175 g/6 oz cream cheese, softened

4 tbsp chopped fresh herbs, such as parsley, dill, chives and basil

1 to 2 spring onions, finely chopped

Salt and freshly ground black pepper, to taste

In a medium bowl, beat the cream cheese with the herbs and spring onions until well blended. Season to taste with salt and pepper. Store as for other spreads.

Basil Butter

makes about 175 g/6 oz

115 g/4 oz butter

4 tbsp extra virgin olive oil

12 large basil leaves

Put the butter, oil and basil leaves in a bowl of a food processor fitted with the metal blade and process for 30 to 60 seconds until well blended, scraping down the side of the bowl once or twice. Store as for other butters.

muffins

VERY BLUE-BLUEBERRY MUFFINS

makes 12 muffins

225 g/8 oz plain flour

2½ tsp baking powder

½ tsp salt

¼ tsp freshly grated or ground nutmeg

175 g/6 oz sugar

2 eggs

175 ml/6 fl oz milk

115 g/4 oz butter or margarine, melted and cooled

Grated rind of ½ orange

1 tsp vanilla essence

50 g/2 oz blueberries, mashed

225 g/8 oz blueberries

50 g/2 oz granulated sugar, mixed with

¼ tsp freshly grated nutmeg

TIP *Muffin cup tins can vary in size, depending on the manufacturer. Your mixture may not completely fill each cup; if so, it doesn't really matter. Whatever the size, make sure to fill the cups about ¾ full.*

These muffins are bursting with blueberries; mashing some of the berries releases more flavour into the batter.

1 Preheat the oven to 190°C/375°F/gas mark 5. Lightly grease or spray a 12-cup muffin tin or line each cup with a paper case. Sift the flour, baking powder, salt and nutmeg into a large bowl; stir in the sugar and make a well in the centre.

2 In another bowl, beat the eggs, milk, melted butter or margarine, grated orange rind and vanilla essence; then stir in the mashed blueberries. Pour into the well and lightly stir using a fork, until blended in. Do not overmix.

Lightly fold in the remaining blueberries.

3 Spoon the mixture into the prepared muffin cups, filling each to almost full. Sprinkle each with the sugar-nutmeg mixture. Bake until risen and golden (a fine skewer or wooden cocktail stick inserted in the centre should come out with a few crumbs attached), 25 to 30 minutes. Remove the tin to a wire rack to cool, about 2 minutes, then remove the muffins to the wire rack to cool. Serve warm or at room temperature.

BUTTERMILK BRAN MUFFINS

makes 24 muffins

275 g/10 oz plain flour

2 ½ tsp bicarbonate of soda

½ tsp salt

275–350 g/10–12 oz bran,
preferably unprocessed

175 g/6 oz raisins

2 eggs

225 g/8 oz sugar

115 g/4 oz butter, melted and
cooled

225 ml/8 fl oz water

450 ml/16 fl oz buttermilk

Buttermilk makes these rich muffins tender and crumbly with a light texture. This mixture can be stored in the refrigerator, then baked fresh as required.

1 Preheat the oven to 190°C/375°F/gas mark 5. Lightly grease or spray two 12-cup muffin tins or line each cup with double paper or foil cases. Sift the flour, bicarbonate of soda and salt into a medium bowl, then stir in the bran and raisins.
2 Using an electric mixer, beat the eggs, sugar and butter in a large bowl until well blended. Slowly beat in the water and buttermilk, but don't worry if the mixture looks curdled. Lightly stir in the flour-bran mixture. Do not overmix; the batter should be slightly lumpy. Cover and refrigerate for at least 30 minutes to allow the bran to absorb some of the moisture. The batter can be stored for up to 4 weeks without losing its freshness.
3 Stir the batter gently to reblend. Scoop the batter into the prepared tins or cases. Bake until risen and well coloured and a fine skewer or wooden cocktail stick inserted in the centre comes out clean, about 25 minutes. Remove the tins to a wire rack to cool, about 2 minutes, then remove muffins to the wire rack to cool, or until just warm and ready to serve.

TIP *Unless you always have buttermilk or yogurt on hand, 1 tablespoon of lemon juice added to 225 ml/8 fl oz of milk makes an easy substitute. Or, if you can find dried buttermilk, reconstitute following the directions on the packet.*

ALMOND AND POPPY SEED MUFFINS

makes 12 muffins

2 tbsp poppy seeds, plus extra for sprinkling

200 g/7 oz plain flour

2 tsp baking powder

½ tsp salt

115 g/4 oz sugar, plus extra for sprinkling

1 egg

175 ml/6 fl oz milk

4 tbsp sunflower or other light vegetable oil or 50 g/2 oz butter or margarine, melted and cooled

½ tsp almond essence

50 g/2 oz whole blanched almonds, lightly toasted and chopped

Poppy seeds add a delicate flavour and slightly crunchy texture to these light, almond-flavoured muffins.

1 Preheat the oven to 190°C/375°F/gas mark 5. Grease or spray a 12-cup muffin tin, or line each cup with paper cases or foil cases. Put 2 tablespoons of the poppy seeds in a bowl and crush lightly with the back of a spoon. Sift in the flour, baking powder and salt, then stir in the sugar until well blended, and make a well in the centre.

2 Beat the egg and milk together in a bowl until well blended. Gradually beat in the oil, melted butter or margarine and the almond essence. Pour into the well, add the chopped almonds and stir lightly or until just blended. Do not overmix; the batter should be slightly lumpy.

3 Spoon the mixture into the prepared tins or cases, filling each about ¾ full. Combine a tablespoon of sugar and one teaspoon of poppy seeds in a small cup; sprinkle a little mixture over the top of each muffin. Bake until risen and golden, and a fine skewer inserted into the centre comes out clean, 20 to 25 minutes. Remove the tin to a wire rack to cool, about 2 minutes, then remove the muffins to a wire rack to cool. Serve warm or at room temperature.

SOURED CREAM AND CHERRY MUFFINS

with cherry compote

makes 12 muffins

75 g/3 oz semi-dried cherries
200 g/7 oz plain flour
1 tsp baking powder
½ tsp bicarbonate of soda
½ tsp salt
½ tsp ground cardamom
115 g/4 oz sugar
1 egg
225 ml/8 fl oz soured cream
½ tsp vanilla essence

These delicious muffins are moist, crumbly and delicately flavoured, and are enhanced by the intense flavour of the cherry compote. A spectacular brunch or dessert recipe.

1 Put the cherries in a small bowl and pour over enough boiling water to cover them. Allow to stand for about 15 minutes to soften. Drain and pat dry with absorbent kitchen paper.

2 Preheat the oven to 200°C/400°F/gas mark 6. Grease or spray a 12-cup muffin tin or line with paper cases. Sift the flour, baking powder, bicarbonate of soda, salt and ground cardamom into a large bowl. Stir in the sugar, then the cherries, being sure they are coated with the flour mixture, and make a well in the centre.

3 Beat the egg and soured cream in another bowl until well blended; beat in the vanilla. Pour into the well and stir lightly until just combined. Do not overmix; the batter should be slightly lumpy.

4 Spoon the batter into the prepared cups, filling each about ¾ full. Bake until risen and golden, about 20 minutes. Remove the tin to a wire rack to cool, about 2 minutes, then remove muffins to the wire rack to cool until just warm. Serve with the Cherry Compote.

cherry compote

makes about 675 g/1½ lb

450 g/1 lb fresh black or red cherries, stoned
225 g/8 oz dried cherries
1 vanilla pod, split
4 to 6 cardamom pods, crushed

115 g/4 oz sugar
1 tsp cornflour or arrowroot, dissolved in
2 tsp cold water

Put the first five ingredients in a large, noncorrosive saucepan, then add just enough water to cover the fruit. Place over medium heat and bring to the boil, stirring to dissolve the sugar. Simmer for about 5 minutes, until the cherries are just tender. Stir the dissolved cornflour or arrowroot, and then stir into the simmering cherry liquid. Bring to the boil and cook for 1 to 2 minutes, until the juices are thickened and clear. Remove from the heat to cool, stirring occasionally. Pour into a bowl and refrigerate, covered, until ready to serve.

DOUBLE CHOCOLATE CHIP MUFFINS

makes 10 muffins
200 g/7 oz plain flour
25 g/1 oz cocoa powder
1 tbsp baking powder
½ tsp salt
115 g/4 oz sugar
75 g/3 oz plain chocolate chips and
40 g/1½ oz white chocolate chips
2 eggs
100 ml/4 fl oz sunflower or
vegetable oil
225 ml/8 fl oz milk
1 tsp vanilla essence

These rich, chocolate muffins make a great morning snack with a cup of cappuccino or a glass of cold milk.

1 Preheat the oven to 200°C/400°F/gas mark 6. Line a 10-cup muffin tin with foil or double-paper cases. Half fill any remaining empty cups in the tin with water to prevent them from scorching. Sift the flour, cocoa powder, baking powder and salt into a bowl. Stir in the sugar and chocolate chips, then make a well in the centre.

2 In another bowl beat the eggs with the oil until foamy. Gradually beat in the milk and vanilla essence. Pour into the well and stir until just combined. Do not overmix; the batter should be slightly lumpy.

3 Spoon the batter into the prepared cups, filling each about ¾ full. Bake until risen, golden and springy when pressed with your fingertip, about 20 minutes. Remove tin to a wire rack to cool, about 2 minutes, then remove muffins to the wire rack to cool. Serve warm or at room temperature.

OATMEAL AND RAISIN MUFFINS

makes 12 muffins

90 g/3½ oz rolled oats

115 g/4 oz plain flour

2 tsp baking powder

½ tsp ground cinnamon

½ tsp salt

75 g/3 oz raisins

50 g/2 oz wholemeal flour

2 eggs

115 g/4 oz dark brown sugar

175 ml/6 fl oz milk

50 g/2 oz butter or margarine,

melted and cooled

½ tsp vanilla essence

Oatmeal adds a chewy texture to these dark, moist muffins. Substitute dried cranberries for raisins, if you like.

1 Preheat the oven to 200°C/400°F/gas mark 6. Grease or spray a 12-cup muffin tin or line with double-paper cases. Put the oats in a large bowl and sift in the plain flour, baking powder, cinnamon and salt. Stir in the raisins and wholemeal flour, then make a well in the centre.

2 Using an electric mixer, beat the eggs and brown sugar in another bowl until foamy. Gradually beat in the milk, melted butter or margarine and vanilla essence until well blended.

Pour into the well and stir until combined. Do not overmix; the batter should be slightly lumpy.

3 Spoon the batter into the prepared cups, filling each about ¾ full. Bake until risen, golden and springy when pressed with your fingertip, about 20 minutes. Remove the tin to a wire rack to cool, then remove the muffins to the rack, about 2 minutes. If you like, serve them with salted butter or a flavoured butter such as Honey and Ginger Butter (see page 28).

WARM ORANGE MUFFINS

with winter dried fruit salad

200 g/7 oz plain flour
2 tsp baking powder
½ tsp salt
115 g/4 oz sugar
75 g/3 oz candied orange peel,
chopped
1 egg
Grated rind of 1 orange
½ tsp vanilla essence
225 ml/8 fl oz buttermilk
50 g/2 oz butter or margarine,
melted and cooled

These warm, delicate muffins make a perfect accompaniment to a 'winter salad' of dried fruits. Serve with fresh whipped cream or crème fraîche for a brunch, snack, dessert or treat.

1 Preheat the oven to 200°C/400°F/gas mark 6. Grease or spray a 12-cup muffin tin or line with paper cases. Sift the flour, baking powder and salt into a large bowl, then stir in the sugar and chopped orange peel, then make a well in the centre.

2 Beat the egg, orange rind and vanilla essence in another bowl until foamy. Beat in the buttermilk and melted butter. Pour into the well and lightly stir until just combined. Do not overmix; the batter should be slightly lumpy.

3 Spoon the batter into the prepared cups, filling each about ¾ full. Bake until risen and golden, and a fine skewer inserted in the centre comes out clean, about 20 minutes. Remove the tin to a wire rack to cool, about 2 minutes, then remove the muffins to the wire rack to cool slightly. Serve warm with the Winter Dried Fruit Salad.

winter dried fruit salad

350 g/12 oz large, stoned prunes
250 g/9 oz dried, no-soak apricots
250 g/9 oz dried, no-soak pears
150 g/5 oz dried, no-soak peaches
75 g/3 oz sultanas or seedless raisins
1 orange

1 tsp vanilla essence
1 cinnamon stick
2 to 3 cloves
2 to 3 tbsp sugar or honey, or to taste
boiling water

Put the prunes, apricots, pears and peaches in a large bowl, then sprinkle in the raisins. Using a swivel-bladed vegetable peeler, peel the orange rind in long, thin strips, and add to the fruit. Cut the orange in half and squeeze the juice over the fruit, removing any seeds. Add the vanilla essence, cinnamon stick, cloves and the sugar or honey to taste. Pour over enough boiling water to cover the fruit by 2.5 cm/1 inch, then cover and allow to stand for at least 1 hour until the fruit is plump and tender. Stir to blend in the flavours (remove the cinnamon stick and cloves if you like), and serve at room temperature or refrigerate to serve chilled.

BERRY FRUIT MUFFINS

with berry fruit compote

makes 12 muffins
200 g/7 oz plain flour
1 tbsp baking powder
½ tsp salt
175 g/6 oz sugar
1 egg
75 g/3 oz butter
100 ml/4 fl oz milk
Grated lemon or orange rind
½ tsp vanilla essence
150 g/5 oz fresh blueberries,
raspberries, black or redcurrants
Whipped cream to serve
Fresh mint sprigs to decorate

Use any combination of summer berries or just one kind if you prefer; if using fresh cherries, these should first be stoned and quartered. Serve with Berry Fruit Compote.

1 Preheat the oven to 200°C/400°F/gas mark 6. Grease or spray a 12-cup muffin tin or line each cup with double paper or foil cases. Sift the flour, baking powder and salt into a bowl, then stir in the sugar and make a well in the centre.

2 In another bowl beat the egg, melted and cooled butter, milk, lemon or orange rind and vanilla essence until well blended. Pour into the well and lightly stir into the flour mixture with a fork. Before the mixture is combined, sprinkle over the berries and fold in very lightly. Do not overmix; the batter should be slightly lumpy.

3 Spoon the mixture into the prepared tin, filling each muffin cup about ⅔ full. Bake until risen and golden, and a fine skewer inserted into the centre comes out clean, 20 to 25 minutes. Remove the pan to a wire rack to cool, about 2 minutes, then remove the muffins to the rack to cool. Serve warm or at room temperature with the Berry Fruit Compote and whipped cream, decorating with fresh mint, if desired.

TIP *Alternatively, combine the fruits, lemon juice and sugar in a microwave-safe bowl. Sprinkle with 2 to 3 tablespoons water and cover. Microwave on high (full power) for 3 to 4 minutes. Serve hot or leave to stand until cool, then refrigerate until chilled, and serve.*

berry fruit compote

This fruit mixture can be served warm or cold, and makes a delicious accompaniment to warm, fruit-filled muffins. Vary the compote with whatever fruits are available.

450 g/1 lb strawberries, cut in half or quarters, if large
450 g/1 lb mixed berries, such as raspberries,
blueberries, blackberries, stoned black or red cherries

Juice of 1 lemon or orange
3 to 4 tbsp sugar, or to taste
100 ml/4 fl oz water

Combine the strawberries and mixed berries in a large, non-corrosive saucepan. Add the lemon or orange juice and sprinkle with the sugar, then pour in the water. Place the pan over medium heat and allow the mixture to simmer; shake the pan gently to lightly mix the fruits. Do not allow the fruit to boil, but cook the fruits until they just begin to soften, about 5 minutes. Remove from the heat and cover until cooled slightly. Refrigerate until chilled.

PECAN MOLASSES CORN MUFFINS

with cured ham

makes 12 normal or
24 mini-muffins

165 g/5½ oz plain flour
2 tsp bicarbonate of soda
1 tsp salt
90 g/3½ oz cornmeal
2 tsp sugar
40 g/1½ oz raisins
50 g/2 oz chopped, toasted pecans
2 eggs
225 ml/8 fl oz soured cream
50 g/2 oz butter, melted and cooled
75 g/3 oz molasses
50 g/2 oz butter for spreading
6 slices good quality cured ham, thinly sliced, such as prosciutto or Virginia ham

These little muffins make a great breakfast snack or lunch. For a mini-muffin, bake the muffin batter in prepared mini-muffin tins, reducing the time to 8 to 10 minutes.

1 Preheat the oven to 200°C/400°F/gas mark 6. Grease or spray a 12-cup muffin tin or line with paper cases. Sift the flour, bicarbonate of soda and salt into a large bowl. Stir in the cornmeal and sugar until blended, then stir in the raisins and pecans until well mixed. Make a well in the centre.
2 In another bowl using an electric mixer, beat the eggs with the soured cream until well blended. Gradually beat in the melted butter and molasses until very well blended. Pour into the well, stirring lightly until combined. Do not overmix; the batter should be slightly lumpy.
3 Spoon the batter into the prepared tins, filling each cup about ⅔ full. Bake until risen, golden and a fine skewer inserted in the centre comes out with just a few crumbs attached, 15 to 20 minutes. Do not overbake or muffins will be dry. Remove to a wire rack to cool, about 2 minutes, then remove muffins to the wire rack to cool to room temperature.
4 To serve as sandwiches, cut each muffin crossways in half, and spread each cut surface with a little softened butter. Cut each ham slice in half lengthways, and arrange a half slice on the bottom half of each muffin. Cover each with its top and serve.

ITALIAN RICE MUFFINS

with honey and amaretto butter

makes 12 muffins
115 g/4 oz plain flour
1 tbsp baking powder
½ tsp bicarbonate of soda
½ tsp salt
1 egg
75 g/3 oz honey
100 ml/4 fl oz milk
2 tbsp sunflower or vegetable oil
½ tsp almond essence
150 g/5 oz cooked rice,
lightly packed
2 Amaretti biscuits, coarsely crushed

These muffins have a delicate flavour and texture. If possible, use a good arborio rice that has a plump grain and cook it until just *al dente* (firm to the bite).

1 Preheat the oven to 200°C/400°F/gas mark 6. Grease or spray a 12-cup muffin tin or line with paper cases. Sift the flour, baking powder, bicarbonate of soda and salt into a large bowl, then make a well in the centre.

2 Beat the egg with the honey in another bowl until well blended and foamy. Gradually beat in the milk, oil and almond essence, then whisk in the rice, separating any lumps. Pour into the well and stir lightly until just combined. Do not overmix; the batter should be slightly lumpy.

3 Spoon the batter into the prepared cups, filling each about ⅔ full. Sprinkle the tops with a little of the Amaretti crumbs. Bake until risen, golden and springy when pressed, 15 to 20 minutes. Remove the tin to a wire rack to cool, about 2 minutes, then remove muffins to the wire rack to cool until just warm. Serve with Honey and Amaretto Butter.

honey and amaretto butter

makes about 175 g/6 oz
115 g/4 oz unsalted butter, softened
2 tbsp honey
2 tbsp Amaretto liqueur

In a small bowl, beat the butter until smooth and creamy, then beat in the honey and Amaretto liqueur until well blended. Spoon onto a piece of greaseproof paper or cling film, and shape into a log about 2.5 cm/1 inch thick. Wrap and refrigerate until chilled, about 1 hour. Cut into rounds to serve; allow to soften for a few minutes at room temperature for easier spreading.

GINGERY PEAR AND PECAN MUFFINS

with honey and ginger butter

makes 18 muffins

225 g/8 oz plain flour

2 tsp baking powder

½ tsp salt

¼ tsp ground cinnamon

175 g/6 oz sugar

2 eggs

100 ml/4 fl oz sunflower or other vegetable oil

2 tbsp milk

1 tsp grated fresh root ginger

2 ripe, medium pears, peeled, cored and chopped

75 g/3 oz pecans, chopped

40 g/1½ oz crystallised or stem ginger, chopped

Ginger and pear go well together, and the combination of tangy, fresh root ginger and sweet, crystallised or stem ginger create a 'hot-and-spicy' sensation.

1 Preheat the oven to 190°C/375°F/gas mark 5. Lightly grease or spray 18-cup muffin tins or line each cup with a paper case. Sift the flour, baking powder, salt and ground cinnamon into a large bowl, then stir in the sugar and make a well in the centre.

2 Beat the eggs, oil, milk and grated fresh ginger in another bowl until well blended. Pour into the well. Using a fork, lightly stir until just combined. Do not overmix; the batter should be slightly lumpy. Gently fold in the pears, pecans and ginger.

3 Spoon the batter into the prepared muffin cups, filling each just over ⅔ full. Bake until risen and golden, and a fine skewer inserted in the centre comes out clean, 20 to 25 minutes. Remove to a wire rack to cool, 2 minutes, then remove the muffins to the wire rack to cool. Serve warm with the Honey and Ginger Butter.

TIP *Chopped nuts, fruit or even chocolate chips can be added at various stages. Tossing them in the dry ingredients before mixing with the liquids helps to even out their distribution, but they can be folded in just before the batter is completed.*

honey and ginger butter

makes about 225 g/8 oz

225 g/8 oz unsalted butter, softened

1 to 2 tbsp honey

½ tsp ground ginger

¼ tsp ground cinnamon

Beat the butter in a medium-sized bowl until light and creamy, about 1 to 2 minutes. Add the honey, ginger and cinnamon, and beat until well blended. Spoon into a bowl and refrigerate, covered, until ready to serve. Soften for a few minutes at room temperature for easier spreading.

CHEESY BACON MUFFINS

with herby spring onion cream cheese spread

makes 12 muffins

6 rashers bacon

Vegetable oil

175 g/6 oz plain flour

2 tsp baking powder

½ tsp salt

2 tsp sugar

115 g/4 oz Swiss, Gruyère or other cheese, grated

3 to 4 spring onions, finely chopped

1 egg

175 ml/6 fl oz milk

1 tbsp Dijon mustard

These savoury muffins are delicious as a brunch dish or with scrambled eggs. Vary the cheese to your taste.

1 Preheat the oven to 200°C/400°F/gas mark 6. Grease or spray 12-cup muffin tins, or line each with paper cases. Put the bacon in a large frying pan and fry over medium heat, turning once, until crisp and brown on both sides. Drain on absorbent kitchen paper, and pour the remaining fat into a cup. Add extra oil, if necessary, to make 4 tablespoons. When cool, crumble the bacon into small pieces.

2 Meanwhile, sift the flour, baking powder and salt into a large bowl. Stir in the sugar, cheese and spring onions, tossing lightly to mix. Add the bacon and mix again, then make a well in the centre.

3 Beat the egg with the milk in another bowl until well blended. Beat in the mustard and the reserved bacon fat. Pour into the well and stir lightly until just combined. Do not overmix; the batter should be slightly lumpy.

4 Spoon the mixture into the prepared muffin cups and bake until risen, golden and springy when pressed, 15 to 20 minutes. Remove to a wire rack to cool, about 2 minutes, then remove the muffins to the rack to cool until just warm. Serve warm with the Herby Spring Onion Cream Cheese Spread (see page 13).

PARMESAN AND PINE NUT MINI-MUFFINS

with sun-dried tomato butter

makes 24 mini-muffins

175 g/6 oz plain flour

2 tsp baking powder

¼ tsp salt

½ tsp dried basil leaves, crumbled

65 g/2½ oz sugar

75 g/3 oz sultanas

50 g/2 oz pine nuts, lightly toasted, plus extra for sprinkling

50 g/2 oz Parmesan cheese

1 egg

175 ml/6 fl oz milk

50 g/2 oz butter, melted and cooled

TIP *If you prefer a larger muffin, bake the batter in a 12-cup muffin tin prepared as above for about 20 minutes.*

These delicious mini-muffins have an unusual, versatile flavour. Served with a tangy sun-dried tomato butter, they make a great savoury snack or *hors d'oeuvre*; with a sweetened honey or cinnamon butter, they have a much sweeter taste. Try them both ways.

1 Preheat the oven to 190°C/375°F/gas mark 5. Grease or spray 24-cup mini-muffin tin or line with mini-paper or foil cases. Sift the flour, baking powder and salt into a large bowl. Stir in the dried basil, sugar, raisins, pine nuts and freshly grated Parmesan until well mixed, then make a well in the centre.

2 Whisk the egg with the milk in another bowl until well blended and foamy, then whisk in the melted butter. Pour into the well and lightly fold together until combined. Do not overmix; the batter should be slightly lumpy.

3 Spoon batter into the prepared cups, filling each to almost full. Sprinkle each with a few pine nuts. Bake until risen, golden and springy when pressed, about 15 minutes. Remove to a wire rack to cool, 1 to 2 minutes, then remove the muffins to the wire rack to cool until just warm. Serve warm with the sun-dried tomato butter. Alternatively, cool to room temperature, then split each muffin crossways, spread the bottom halves with the butter and sandwich together.

sun-dried tomato butter

makes about 275 g/10 oz

175 g/6 oz unsalted butter, softened

115 g/4 oz sun-dried tomatoes, packed in oil, drained and chopped

Freshly ground black pepper

In a medium bowl, beat the butter until smooth and creamy. Add the sun-dried tomatoes and season with pepper to taste. Stir gently until well blended. Scrape into a serving bowl and refrigerate, covered, until ready to serve. Soften for a few minutes at room temperature for easier spreading.

scones and bakes

TEA SCONES

with cream and jam

makes about 15 scones

350 g / 12 oz plain flour

1 ½ tsp bicarbonate of soda

½ tsp salt

3 tbsp sugar

75 g / 3 oz unsalted butter,

cut into pieces

50 g / 2 oz seedless currants or

raisins

1 egg, lightly beaten

275 ml / ½ pint buttermilk

2 tbsp milk

Clotted cream or lightly whipped

double cream to serve

Jam to serve

This recipe uses buttermilk which makes the scones soft and fluffy, with a smooth texture.

1 Preheat the oven to 220°C/425°F/gas mark 7. Lightly flour a large baking sheet. Sift the flour, bicarbonate of soda and salt into a large bowl, then stir in the sugar.

2 Sprinkle the butter pieces over the flour mixture. Rub in the butter until the mixture resembles medium crumbs. Blend in the currants or raisins and make a well in the centre.

3 Beat the egg with 175 ml/6 fl oz of the buttermilk in a small bowl, then pour into the well. Stir the flour mixture into the liquid with a fork until it is combined. Do not overmix. Form the dough into a rough ball and place on a lightly floured surface: knead lightly 8 to 10 times until blended.

4 Roll or pat the dough into a 2-cm/¾-inch thick round. Use a floured, 6.5-cm/2½-inch wide, round cutter to cut out as many rounds as possible. Transfer to the baking sheet, arranging them about 2.5-cm/1 inch apart. Press the trimmings together and shape into another 2-cm/¾-inch thick round, then cut out as many 6.5-cm/2½-inch thick rounds as possible. Transfer these to the baking sheet.

5 Brush the tops of the scones with a little milk and bake until risen and golden, about 15 minutes. Remove the scones to a wire rack to cool slightly. Serve warm with fresh, whipped cream and raspberry or strawberry jam.

TIP *When cutting out the scones, cut straight down, do not twist the cutter, or the scones will rise unevenly.*

CRANBERRY ORANGE SCONES

with cranberry and raspberry butter

makes about 10 scones
350 g/12 oz plain flour
1 tbsp baking powder
½ tsp salt
2 tbsp sugar, plus
extra for sprinkling
Grated rind of 1 orange
50 g/2 oz unsalted butter,
cut into pieces
115 g/4 oz dried cranberries
2 eggs
100–150 ml/4–5 fl oz double
cream, plus extra for glazing
½ tsp vanilla essence
2 tbsp milk
2 tbsp light brown sugar

TIP *If the cranberries are very dry, plump them by covering with boiling water; stand for 5 minutes, then drain and pat dry with absorbent kitchen paper.*

These delicious, orange-flavoured scones are filled with chewy, dried cranberries. If you like, use dried cherries instead, and serve with cherry compote (see page 18).

1 Preheat the oven to 220°C/425°F/gas mark 7. Lightly flour a large baking sheet. Sift the flour, baking powder and salt into a large bowl; stir in the sugar and the grated orange rind.
2 Sprinkle the butter pieces over the flour mixture and rub in the butter using a pastry blender or your fingertips, until the mixture resembles medium crumbs. Stir in the dried cranberries and make a well in the centre.
3 In a small bowl, beat the egg and 100 ml/ 4 fl oz of the cream until blended; beat in the vanilla essence and pour into the well. Using a fork, stir the flour mixture into the liquid just until it begins to combine; do not overmix. Form dough into a rough ball and place on a lightly floured surface. Knead 6 to 8 times until blended.

cranberry and raspberry butter

makes about 225 g/8 oz
175 g/6 oz unsalted butter, softened
1 tbsp cranberry sauce
1 tbsp raspberry jam

Beat the butter until smooth and creamy in a small bowl. Beat in the cranberry sauce, raspberry jam, orange juice and ground

Pat the dough into a 2-cm/¾-inch thick round and cut out as many rounds as possible using a 6.5-cm/2½-inch floured cutter. Transfer to the baking sheet, arranging them about 2.5-cm/1-inch apart. Press the trimmings together and roll or pat to another 2-cm/¾-inch thick round, then cut out as many rounds as possible. Transfer to the baking sheet.
4 Brush the top of the scones with a little more cream or milk, then sprinkle with sugar. Bake until risen and golden, about 12 minutes. Remove to a wire rack to cool, about 3 to 4 minutes, then transfer scones onto the wire rack to cool until just warm. Serve with Cranberry and Raspberry Butter.

1 tbsp orange juice
½ tsp ground cinnamon

cinnamon until well blended. Scrape into a serving bowl and refrigerate, covered, until ready to serve.

COUNTRY APPLE SCONES

makes 8 scones

scant 200 g/7 oz flour

1½ tsp baking powder

½ tsp bicarbonate of soda

½ tsp salt

½ tsp ground cinnamon

115 g/4 oz sugar

Grated rind of 1 orange

50 g/2 oz butter, cut into pieces

2 small dessert apples, peeled, cored and chopped

100–175 ml/4–6 fl oz buttermilk

½ tsp vanilla essence

2 tbsp brown sugar

2 tbsp flaked almonds

These rustic-looking scones are packed with flavour, and because they are long-lasting and substantial, make a cold weather treat.

1 Preheat the oven to 200°C/400°F/gas mark 6. Lightly flour a large baking sheet. Sift the flour, baking powder, bicarbonate of soda, salt and cinnamon into a large bowl; stir in the sugar and the grated orange rind.

2 Sprinkle the butter pieces over the flour mixture, then rub in the butter using a pastry blender or your fingertips until the mixture resembles coarse breadcrumbs. Stir in the apples, tossing to coat well with the flour mixture, and make a well in the centre.

3 Pour in most of the buttermilk and the vanilla essence, then stir lightly with a fork until a soft dough forms. Add more buttermilk if the dough seems too dry, but do not overmix. Form the dough into a rough ball and place on a lightly floured surface; knead 8 to 10 times to blend. Pat the dough into a 2-cm/¾-inch thick round, about 20 cm/8 inches in diameter, and transfer to the baking sheet.

4 Brush the top of the dough with the remaining buttermilk and sprinkle with the brown sugar and almonds. Using a sharp knife, score the top deeply into eight wedges. Do not drag the knife through, but wiggle it to separate each edge by about 1cm/½ inch. Bake until risen and golden, 15 to 20 minutes. Remove to a wire rack to cool, about 2 minutes, then transfer to the wire rack to cool to room temperature. Serve warm with raspberry or strawberry jam.

TIP *When making scones, avoid over-mixing the fat and flour. Use chilled butter or margarine, and rub these in until the mixture resembles coarse to fine breadcrumbs.*

WALNUT AND DATE SCONES

with sweet date butter

makes 8 scones

75 g/3 oz plain flour

75 g/3 oz wholemeal flour and
a little extra for dusting

4 tsp baking powder

½ tsp salt

½ tsp ground cinnamon

40 g/1½ oz light brown sugar

25 g/1 oz butter, cut into pieces

50 g/2 oz chopped walnuts,
lightly toasted

75 g/3 oz chopped dates

100–175 ml/4–6 fl oz milk

These dark, dense scones are delicious and moist, and make a substantial breakfast with a bowl of yogurt drizzled with honey.

1 Preheat the oven to 220°C/425°F/gas mark 7. Lightly flour a large baking sheet. Sift the flours, baking powder, salt and cinnamon into a large bowl; stir in the brown sugar.

2 Sprinkle the butter pieces over the flour. Rub in the butter using a pastry blender or your fingertips, until the mixture resembles coarse breadcrumbs. Stir in the walnuts and dates, and make a well in the centre. Add 100 ml/4 fl oz milk and stir until a soft dough forms, adding a little more milk if necessary. Form into a rough ball.

3 Place on a lightly floured surface and knead once or twice. Roll out or pat into a 2-cm/¾-inch thick square. Using a sharp knife dipped in flour, cut straight down into 8 to 9 squares, but do not drag the knife or the scones will rise unevenly. Transfer the scones to the baking sheet, arranging them about 2.5 cm/1 inch apart. Press the trimmings together and roll or pat into another 2-cm/¾-inch thick square. Cut out as many squares as possible and transfer to the baking sheet.

4 Dust the tops with a little wholemeal flour and bake until risen and golden, 10 to 12 minutes. Remove to a wire rack and cool, about 2 minutes, then transfer the scones to the wire rack to cool until just warm, and serve with Sweet Date Butter if desired (see page 12).

LEMON CREAM SCONES

with fresh lemon curd

makes 9 scones

225 g/8 oz plain flour

1 tbsp baking powder

½ tsp salt

65 g/2½ oz sugar

115 g/4 oz dried apricots, chopped

Grated rind of 1 large lemon

about 275 ml/½ pint double cream for whipping

Icing sugar for dusting

Whipped cream to serve (optional)

These sweet scones are moist and crumbly, and have a wonderful flavour. The fresh lemon curd is a luscious extra. The scones are equally delicious with a good quality apricot jam.

1 Preheat the oven to 220°C/425°F/gas mark 7. Lightly flour a large baking sheet. Sift the flour, baking powder and salt into a large bowl. Stir in the sugar, dried apricots and grated lemon rind, then make a well in the centre.

2 Add most of the cream, and stir lightly until a soft dough forms, adding a little more cream if necessary. Form into a rough ball and place on a lightly floured surface. Knead 5 to 6 times until just combined. Roll or pat dough into a 2-cm/¾-inch square about 20 x 20 cm/8 x 8 inches.

Cut into 9 squares. Alternatively, use a floured 6.5–7.5-cm/2½ to 3-inch cutter to cut into rounds (see Tea Scones, page 33).

3 Arrange the squares or rounds on the baking sheet, about 2.5 cm/1 inch apart. Bake until risen and golden, 10 to 14 minutes. Remove to a wire rack to cool, about 2 minutes, then transfer the scones to the wire rack to cool to room temperature. Dust lightly with icing sugar and serve warm with the lemon curd and whipped cream, if using.

fresh lemon curd

makes about 450 g/1 lb

Grated rind and juice of 1 large lemon

175 g/6 oz unsalted butter, cut into pieces

225 g/8 oz sugar

¼ tsp salt

3 eggs, lightly beaten

Put the grated lemon rind, lemon juice, butter, sugar and salt in the top of a heatproof bowl. Place over a saucepan of just simmering water; heat over low heat until the butter melts, stirring frequently.

Whisk the eggs into the butter mixture and cook over low heat until the mixture thickens, about 15 minutes. Do not allow to boil, or the mixture will curdle. Pour or strain into a bowl, then press a piece of cling film directly against the surface to prevent a skin from forming. Refrigerate until chilled, and ready to serve.

SESAME AND ROQUEFORT CRESCENTS

makes 12 crescents

250 g/9 oz plain flour

2 tsp baking powder

½ tsp salt

¼ tsp bicarbonate of soda

¼ tsp ground ginger

115 g/4 oz white vegetable fat

175 ml/6 fl oz buttermilk

25 g/1 oz butter, melted

50 g/2 oz Roquefort or other strong blue cheese, crumbled

2 tbsp chopped fresh parsley

Sesame seeds for sprinkling

These unusual bakes are shaped like a croissant, and make a delicious alternative to sweeter choices.

1 Preheat the oven to 220°C/425°F/gas mark 7. Lightly grease a large baking sheet. Sift the flour, baking powder, salt, bicarbonate of soda and ground ginger into a large bowl. Add the vegetable fat and using a pastry blender or your fingertips, rub into the flour until the mixture resembles coarse breadcrumbs. Make a well in the centre.

2 Pour in the buttermilk and stir lightly with a fork until just moistened. Form into a rough ball and place on a lightly floured surface. Gently knead 8 to 10 times until just smooth. Using a lightly floured rolling pin, roll into a 0.5-cm/ ¼-inch thick round, about 30 cm/12 inches in diameter. Brush the dough with half the melted butter, then sprinkle with the crumbled cheese and chopped parsley. Using a sharp knife, cut into 12 wedges. Starting from each wide end, roll the dough towards the point.

3 Arrange the crescents, with their points tucked under, on the baking sheet (preferably nonstick), about 5 cm/2 inches apart, pulling the ends toward the centre to form a crescent shape. Sprinkle with the sesame seeds. Bake until puffed and golden, 15 to 20 minutes. Remove to a wire rack and cool for 2 to 3 minutes, then transfer the crescents to the wire rack to cool until just warm.

GOAT'S CHEESE AND SUN-DRIED
TOMATO SCONES *with basil butter*

makes 10 to 12 scones

225 g/8 oz plain flour

2 tsp baking powder

¼ tsp bicarbonate of soda

¼ tsp salt

Freshly ground black pepper

1 to 2 spring onions,
finely chopped

50 g/2 oz chopped, sun-dried
tomatoes, packed in oil, drained

115 g/4 oz semi-soft goat's cheese,
crumbled or diced

1 egg

100–175 ml/4–6 fl oz buttermilk

Serve these delicious scones instead of bread with a tossed salad or pasta dish with a difference. The Basil Butter (see page 13) is good on just about anything.

1 Preheat the oven to 200°C/400°F/gas mark 6. Lightly flour a large baking sheet. Sift the flour, baking powder, bicarbonate of soda and salt into a bowl. Add a few grinds of black pepper, the spring onions, sun-dried tomatoes and goat's cheese and stir well, being sure to coat the tomatoes and cheese, then make a well in the centre.

2 In a small bowl beat the egg with 100 ml/ 4 fl oz buttermilk and pour into the well. Using a fork, stir lightly until just combined, adding a little more buttermilk if necessary. Form into a rough ball and turn onto a lightly floured surface. Knead lightly 6 to 8 times until just smooth.

3 Roll or pat dough into a 2-cm/¾-inch thick circle about 25 cm/10 inches in diameter. Transfer to a baking sheet and using a long-bladed, sharp, floured knife, score deeply into 10 or 12 wedges. Do not drag the knife through the dough or it will not rise evenly.

4 Dust lightly with a little flour and bake until risen and golden, 15 to 18 minutes. Remove to a wire rack to cool 2 to 3 minutes, then slide the scones onto the wire rack to cool until just warm. Serve warm with the Basil Butter.

SWEET POTATO PINWHEELS

with cinnamon, nuts and raisins

makes 10 to 12 pinwheels

175 g/6 oz plain flour

2½ tsp baking powder

½ tsp salt

1 tsp ground cinnamon

75 g/3 oz butter, cut into pieces

1 to 2 tbsp brown sugar

115 g/4 oz cooked sweet potato, mashed

75–100 ml/3–4 fl oz milk

25 g/1 oz butter, melted

filling

50 g/2 oz brown sugar

25 g/1 oz pecans or walnuts, chopped

40 g/1½ oz raisins, chopped

½ tsp ground cinnamon

These delicious bakes are like a slightly sticky, sweet bun, and are great served with morning coffee. The nuts and raisins add a crunchy texture to the warm, spicy-flavoured pinwheels.

1 Preheat the oven to 220°C/425°F/gas mark 7. Lightly grease a large baking sheet. Sift the flour, baking powder, salt and cinnamon into a large bowl. Sprinkle over the butter pieces and rub in using a pastry blender until the mixture resembles coarse breadcrumbs. Stir in the brown sugar and make a well in the centre.

2 Put the sweet potato in a small bowl and whisk in the milk until smooth. Pour into the well, stirring lightly until a soft dough forms. Form into a rough ball.

3 Place on a lightly floured surface and knead lightly 8 to 10 times. Using a lightly floured rolling pin, roll the dough to a 0.5-cm/¼-inch thick rectangle about 25–30 cm/10–12 inches wide, then brush with the melted butter. Combine the filling ingredients in a small bowl and sprinkle over the dough. Starting at one long end, roll the dough, Swiss-roll style. Cut into 2.5-cm/1-inch slices and arrange cut-side down on the baking

sheet, about 1-cm/ ½ inch apart.

4 Bake until puffed and golden, about 12 minutes. Remove to a wire rack to cool slightly, then transfer the pinwheels to the wire rack to cool. Serve warm.

TIP *Scones and these kind of bakes should never be over-mixed or over-kneaded, as they will be tough-textured. Also, cut as many shapes as possible from the first rolling of the dough; extra flour and rerolling may cause drier, tougher results.*

DILL DROP SCONES

with smoked salmon spread

makes 12 scones
225 g/8 oz plain flour
2½ tsp baking powder
¼ tsp salt
75 g/3 oz butter, cut into pieces
2 tsp chopped chives or
spring onions
2 tbsp freshly chopped dill
Freshly ground black pepper
175 g/6 oz cottage cheese
150 ml/¼ pint milk

These savoury scones have a fresh, dill flavour, which is the perfect complement for the rich, full-flavoured smoked salmon spread. Alternatively, fill with smoked salmon strips and serve with scrambled eggs for a delicious lunch or light supper.

1 Preheat the oven to 220°C/425°F/gas mark 7. Line a large baking sheet with foil and lightly grease or spray. Sift the flour, baking powder and salt into a large bowl.

2 Sprinkle the butter pieces over the flour and rub in the butter using a pastry blender or your fingertips until the mixture resembles coarse breadcrumbs. Stir in the chopped chives or spring onions, dill and a few grinds of pepper, stirring until well blended, and make a well in the centre. Pour the cottage cheese and milk into the well and using a fork, stir until just combined.

3 Drop heaped tablespoonfuls onto the prepared baking sheet about 2.5 cm/1 inch apart. Bake until risen and golden, about 15 minutes. Remove to a wire rack to cool about 2 minutes, then remove the scones to the rack to cool to warm or room temperature. Serve with the creamy Smoked Salmon Spread.

smoked salmon spread

The trimmings or off-cuts of smoked salmon are ideal for making this tasty spread.

makes about 350 g/12 oz
175 g/6 oz cream cheese, softened
115 g/4 oz smoked salmon, cut into pieces
1 tbsp freshly squeezed lemon juice
2 tbsp chopped chives or spring onions

2 tbsp chopped fresh dill
Freshly ground black pepper
2 to 4 tbsp double or whipping cream

Put the cream cheese, smoked salmon, lemon juice, spring onions, dill and a few grinds of black pepper into the bowl of a food processor fitted with the metal blade. Process for 30 to 60 seconds until well blended. With the machine running, add the cream, a tablespoon at a time until the mixture is a soft spreadable consistency. Adjust seasoning if necessary. Scrape into a bowl and refrigerate, covered, until ready to serve.

quick breads
and
tea breads

BANANA PECAN LOAF

with chocolate chips

makes 10 servings

scant 75 g/3 oz plain flour

1 tsp bicarbonate of soda

½ tsp salt

1 tsp ground cinnamon

½ tsp ground ginger

scant 75 g/3 oz wholemeal flour

115 g/4 oz butter, softened

scant 175 g/6 oz sugar

2 large ripe bananas, mashed

2 eggs, lightly beaten

5 tbsp just boiling water

115 g/4 oz pecans, chopped

175 g/6 oz plain chocolate chips

for the glaze

65 g/2½ oz icing sugar

2 to 3 tbsp lemon juice

This delicious quick bread is great while the chocolate is still soft and melty, but keeps really well wrapped in cling film or foil.

1 Preheat the oven to 170°C/325°F/gas mark 3. Grease and flour a 23 × 13-cm/9 × 5-inch loaf tin. Sift the flour, bicarbonate of soda, salt, cinnamon and ginger into a medium bowl and stir in the wholemeal flour; set aside.

2 In a large bowl with an electric mixer, beat the butter until light and creamy, 1 to 2 minutes. Gradually beat in the sugar until light and fluffy. On low speed, beat in the mashed bananas and then the eggs; do not worry if the mixture looks curdled. Stir in the flour alternately in batches with the hot water until just combined. Stir in the pecans and chocolate chips.

3 Scrape the mixture into the prepared tin, smoothing the top evenly. Bake until well risen and dark golden brown, about 1 hour 10 minutes. Because this is a very moist quick bread, a fine skewer will not come out clean. Remove the tin to a wire rack to cool for about 30 minutes, then turn out onto the rack, top-side up. To glaze, stir the icing sugar and lemon juice together until smooth. Drizzle over the loaf and allow to set completely.

CHOCOLATE CHIP AND PEANUT BUTTER BREAD

makes 8 to 10 servings

225 g/8 oz plain flour

2 tsp baking powder

¼ tsp salt

175 g/6 oz plain chocolate chips

175 g/6 oz smooth or chunky peanut butter, at room temperature

1 egg, lightly beaten

225 ml/8 fl oz milk

1 tsp vanilla essence

for the chocolate crumb topping

115 g/4 oz sugar

25 g/1 oz cocoa powder

40 g/1½ oz unsalted butter, cut into pieces

2 tbsp finely chopped, dry roasted peanuts

This is a moist, dense bread with a good, peanutty flavour. The chocolate crumb topping is partly layered into the mixture for an extra rich chocolate taste.

1 Preheat the oven to 180°C/350°F/gas mark 4. Lightly grease or spray an 23 x 13-cm/9 x 5 inch loaf tin. Sift the flour, baking powder and salt into a large bowl. Stir in the chocolate chips and make a well in the centre.

2 Put the peanut butter in another bowl and beat with an electric mixer to break up and soften. Gradually beat in the sugar, the egg, milk and vanilla essence. Pour into the well and lightly stir with a fork until combined.

3 Combine the crumb topping ingredients in a small bowl. Spoon half the mixture into the prepared tin and smooth, sprinkling with half of the crumb mixture. Spoon the remaining mixture into the pan and gently smooth the top. Sprinkle with the remaining crumb mixture. Using a round-bladed knife or spoon handle, gently draw through the mixture in a zigzag pattern to give the mixture a slight marbling.

4 Bake until risen and golden, and a fine skewer inserted in the centre comes out moist, but with no uncooked crumbs attached, 50 to 55 minutes. Remove to a wire rack to cool, about 25 minutes, then carefully turn out onto a wire rack, top-side up. Cool completely, then wrap and keep for 1 day before serving, if possible.

FIESTA BUTTERMILK CORNBREAD

makes 8 servings

75 g/3 oz unsalted butter

150 g/5 oz cornmeal

115 g/4 oz plain flour

1½ tsp baking powder

½ tsp bicarbonate of soda

2 tbsp sugar

½ tsp crumbled sage or dried oregano

2 eggs

225 ml/8 fl oz buttermilk

2 to 3 spring onions, finely chopped

1 small red pepper, deseeded and chopped

175 g/6 oz fresh, frozen (thawed) or canned sweetcorn kernels, drained

1 small green chilli, deseeded and chopped (or to taste)

Cornbread is a staple of the American South. This delicious version is flecked with colourful spring onions, red pepper, sweetcorn kernels and even fresh chillies. A delicious accompaniment to Chilli con Carne and other Mexican dishes.

1 Preheat the oven to 200°C/400°F/gas mark 6. Put the butter in a 23-cm/9-inch black iron skillet or heavy 23-cm/9-inch cake tin and place on the middle rack of the oven until butter is melted. Keep pan warm.

2 In a bowl, stir together the cornmeal, flour, baking powder, bicarbonate of soda, sugar and sage or oregano, then make a well in the centre.

3 In a small bowl using a fork, beat the eggs with the buttermilk until well blended. Pour into the well, add all but 2 tablespoons of the melted butter, and stir until just combined. Fold in the onions, pepper, sweetcorn and chilli, until just blended.

4 Pour the mixture into the hot pan or tin and spread evenly. Bake until risen and golden, and a fine skewer inserted into the centre comes out with just a few crumbs attached, about 30 minutes. (Do not overbake or cornbread will be dry.) Remove to a wire rack and cool in the pan or tin, 5 to 10 minutes. Serve hot or warm from the pan or tin with lots of butter, on its own, or as an accompaniment to chilli con carne.

CRANBERRY, APRICOT AND BANANA BREAD

with cranberry apricot compote

makes 8 to 10 servings

150 g/5 oz plain flour

1½ tsp baking powder

½ tsp freshly grated or ground nutmeg

50 g/2 oz rolled oats

175 g/6 oz light brown sugar

75 g/3 oz dried cranberries

75 g/3 oz dried apricots, chopped

2 eggs

100 ml/4 fl oz sunflower or vegetable oil

1 tsp vanilla essence

2 ripe bananas, mashed

The flavours of this moist, delicious tea bread are accentuated by the Cranberry Apricot Compote—a quick, warm preserve.

1 Preheat the oven to 180°C/350°F/gas mark 4. Lightly grease and flour a 20 × 10-cm/8 × 4-inch loaf tin. Sift the flour, baking powder and nutmeg into a bowl. Stir in the oats, brown sugar, cranberries and apricots until well blended, then make a well in the centre.

2 Using an electric mixer in a medium bowl, beat the eggs, oil, vanilla essence, and mashed bananas until well blended. Pour into the well and stir until combined. Scrape the mixture into the prepared tin, smoothing the top evenly.

3 Bake until well risen and golden brown, and a fine skewer inserted in the centre comes out with just a crumb or two attached, about 1 hour. Remove to a wire rack to cool, about 10 minutes, then turn out, top-side up, onto the rack to cool completely.

4 If glazing, in a small bowl, stir the icing sugar and 2 to 3 tablespoons lemon juice until it reaches a pouring consistency. Add a little more lemon juice or water if necessary. Drizzle over the top of the tea bread and allow to set. Alternatively, dust with icing sugar. Serve slices with the Cranberry Apricot Compote.

for glaze (optional)

25 g/1 oz icing sugar

2 to 3 tbsp lemon juice or water

cranberry apricot compote

makes about 450 g/1 lb

50 g/2 oz fresh or frozen cranberries

75 g/3 oz dried cranberries

275–350 g/10–12 oz dried, 'no-soak' apricots, chopped

115 g/4 oz sugar

1 cinnamon stick

Grated rind and juice of 1 orange

2 tbsp ruby port or marsala wine

1 tsp vanilla essence

Put the dried fruits, sugar, cinnamon stick, grated orange rind and juice in a medium heavy-based, noncorrosive saucepan. Add enough water to cover the fruit. Place over medium heat and bring to the boil. Simmer over low heat until the cranberries pop, the fruits are tender and almost all the liquid is absorbed. Remove from the heat, discard the cinnamon stick, stir in the port or marsala and vanilla. Pour into a bowl and serve warm, or refrigerate, covered, until ready to serve.

GINGERBREAD

with whipped cream

makes 9 servings

225 g/8 oz plain flour

2 tsp baking powder

1½ tsp bicarbonate of soda

½ tsp salt

1 tsp ground cinnamon

1 tsp ground ginger

½ tsp freshly grated or

ground nutmeg

¼ tsp ground cloves

⅛ tsp freshly ground black pepper

115 g/4 oz butter or margarine,

softened

50 g/2 oz sugar

175 g/6 oz treacle

(preferably dark)

75 g/3 oz honey

1 egg, lightly beaten

1 tsp vanilla essence

100 ml/4 fl oz buttermilk

Whipped cream to serve

This dark, spicy quick bread brings back childhood memories; it was one of the only occasions we were allowed lots of thick, whipped cream. I still love it.

1 Preheat the oven to 180°C/350°F/gas mark 4. Grease and flour a 23-cm/9-inch square cake tin. Sift the flour, baking powder, bicarbonate of soda, salt, all the spices and pepper into a bowl.

2 In a large bowl with an electric mixer, beat the butter and sugar until light and fluffy, for 1 or 2 minutes. On low speed, beat in the treacle and honey until well blended, scraping down the side of the bowl once, beat in the egg and vanilla essence.

3 Lightly stir in the flour mixture and buttermilk alternately in batches until well blended. Scrape the mixture into the tin and bake until risen and golden, and a fine skewer comes out with just a crumb or two attached, 35 to 40 minutes. Remove to a wire rack to cool, about 10 minutes, then turn out onto the rack, top-side up. Serve warm with thick, whipped cream flavoured with maple syrup, if you like.

CARROT CAKE LOAF

with pistachios

makes 2 loaves of 10
servings each

275 g/10 oz plain flour

2 tsp baking powder

½ tsp bicarbonate of soda

½ tsp salt

*½ tsp freshly grated or
ground nutmeg*

½ tsp ground ginger

*50 g/2 oz toasted wheatgerm or
bran*

115 g/4 oz pistachios, chopped

75 g/3 oz sultanas

3 eggs

225 g/8 oz sugar

75 g/3 oz light brown sugar

*115 g/4 oz butter, melted
and cooled*

225 g/8 oz carrots, grated

Icing sugar for dusting

Grated carrots keep this quick bread sweet and moist, and the pistachios give it a deliciously nutty flavour.

1 Preheat the oven to 180°C/350°F/gas mark 4. Grease a 23 x 13-cm/9 x 5-inch loaf tin. Line the bottom with nonstick baking parchment and grease again, then dust lightly with flour. Sift the flour, baking powder, bicarbonate of soda, salt, nutmeg and ginger into a large bowl; stir in the toasted wheatgerm or bran, pistachios and raisins until well blended, then make a well in the centre.

2 Beat the eggs and sugars together in another bowl with an electric mixer until light and foamy. Beat in the melted butter on low speed, then stir in the grated carrots. Pour into the well and stir with a fork until combined. Do not overmix; the mixture should be slightly lumpy.

3 Pour the mixture into the pan, smoothing the top evenly. Bake until well risen and golden, and a fine skewer inserted in the centre comes out with only a crumb or two attached, about 1 hour. (Cover the tin with foil if the bread colours too quickly.) Remove to a wire rack to cool, about 10 minutes, then turn out, top-side up, to cool completely. Dust lightly with icing sugar before serving.

PASSIONFRUIT-GLAZED CAKE

with orange slices

makes 8 to 10 servings

175 g/6 oz plain flour

¾ tsp baking powder

175 g/6 oz unsalted butter,

softened

225 g/8 oz sugar

Grated rind of 1 small orange

1 tsp vanilla essence

3 eggs, lightly beaten

passionfruit glaze

8 to 10 ripe passionfruits

About 75 g/3 oz sugar

4 seedless oranges, peeled

and segmented

Icing sugar for dusting (optional)

The flavour of this cake comes from the intensity of the passionfruit glaze. Be sure to use the blackest, most wrinkled fruits, as they are usually the ripest.

1 Preheat the oven to 180°C/350°F/gas mark 4. Grease a 23 x 13-cm/9 x 5-inch loaf tin. Line the bottom with nonstick baking parchment. Grease the paper and dust the pan lightly with flour. Sift the flour and baking powder into a bowl.

2 Beat the butter until light and creamy, for 1 to 2 minutes in a large bowl with an electric mixer. Gradually beat in the sugar until light and fluffy, then beat in the grated orange rind and vanilla essence. Beat in the eggs on low speed until well blended. Fold the flour mixture into the egg mixture, until just blended. Scrape into the tin, smoothing the top evenly.

3 Bake until risen and golden, and a fine skewer inserted into the centre comes out clean, about 1 hour. (Cover the top with foil if the cake browns too quickly.) Remove to a wire rack to cool, about 20 minutes.

4 To prepare the glaze, cut six of the passionfruits crossways in half, then scoop the pulp into a nylon sieve or strainer placed over a medium bowl and press through with a wooden spoon. Stir in about 75 g/3 oz sugar; the amount required will depend on the sweetness of the passionfruits. Stir until the sugar is dissolved.

5 Using a long wooden or metal skewer, pierce holes from the top to bottom all over the cake (about 30 holes). Slowly spoon over the glaze and allow to stand for about 20 minutes. Carefully turn out onto the rack, top-side up. If you like, dust with icing sugar before serving.

6 Meanwhile, cut the remaining passionfruits crossways in half, and then scoop the pulp into a bowl; sweeten to taste with 2 to 3 tablespoons of sugar. Serve slices of the cake with a few orange segments drizzled with the passionfruit glaze.

SWEET POLENTA CAKE

with caramelised apples

makes 6 to 8 servings

75 g/3 oz plain flour

65 g/2½ oz polenta or yellow
cornmeal

1 tsp baking powder

Grated rind of 1 lemon

¼ tsp salt

2 eggs

175 g/6 oz sugar

5 tbsp milk

½ tsp almond essence

40 g/1½ oz currants or raisins,
soaked in hot water for 20
minutes, and well drained

75 g/3 oz unsalted butter, softened

2 dessert apples, peeled, cored
and thinly sliced

25 g/1 oz flaked almonds

3 to 4 tbsp apricot jam

Whipped cream, soured cream or
ice cream to serve (optional)

This cake is a slightly more upmarket version of a sweet cornbread—there are many versions found all over Italy.

1 Preheat the oven to 190°C/375°F/gas mark 5. Generously butter a 23-cm/9-inch spring clip tin, then dust the tin lightly with flour. Stir the flour, polenta or cornmeal, baking powder, grated lemon rind, and salt together in a large bowl.
2 Beat the eggs and 115 g/4 oz of the sugar in another bowl with an electric mixer until foamy; gradually beat in the milk and almond essence. Stir in the drained currants or raisins. Beat in the dry ingredients on low speed, adding 4 tablespoons of the softened butter.
3 Spoon into the prepared tin and smooth the top evenly. Arrange the apple slices in concentric circles over the top, and sprinkle with the almonds. In a small saucepan, melt the remaining

butter over low heat and drizzle over the apples. Sprinkle with the remaining sugar.
4 Bake until the cake is puffed and golden, and the apples are lightly caramelised, about 45 minutes. Remove to a wire rack to cool, about 20 minutes. Run a thin knife blade between the cake edge and pan side, then unclip the pan side and carefully remove. Heat the apricot jam with 1 to 2 tablespoons of water in a small saucepan until melted and smooth. Carefully brush or spoon over the top of the apples to glaze. Allow to cool to room temperature. Serve with whipped cream, soured cream or ice cream, as preferred.

TIP: *Be sure to stir or sift together the dry ingredients (including any grated or ground spices) until they are completely well blended. Most wet ingredients can be beaten until well blended with a hand whisk or fork. Heavier mixtures that include mashed bananas, pumpkin or sweet potato might require a hand-held electric mixer.*

PUMPKIN, OATMEAL AND NUT LOAF

with orange lemon butter

makes 2 loaves of 14
servings each
375 g/13 oz plain flour
2 tsp bicarbonate of soda
1 tsp ground cinnamon
½ tsp ground ginger
½ tsp freshly grated or
ground nutmeg
¼ tsp ground cloves
½ tsp salt
75 g/3 oz rolled oats
115 g/4 oz chopped walnuts or
pecans, lightly toasted
One 425–450-g/15–16-oz can
pumpkin
3 eggs, lightly beaten
350 g/12 oz sugar
250 g/9 oz light brown sugar
100 ml/4 fl oz sunflower or
vegetable oil
100 ml/4 fl oz milk
100 ml/4 fl oz evaporated milk

This tea bread has a sweet, natural flavour and lots of texture. Serve with Orange Lemon Butter, or on its own.

1 Preheat the oven to 180°C/350°F/gas mark 4. Grease and flour two 23 × 13-cm/9 × 5-inch loaf tins. Sift the flour, bicarbonate of soda, cinnamon, ginger, nutmeg, cloves and salt into a bowl. Stir in the oats and chopped nuts into the mixture.
2 Put the pumpkin in a large bowl and beat to break up with an electric mixer on low speed. Gradually beat in the eggs until smooth. Beat in the sugars, oil and milks until smooth. On low speed, beat the flour mixture into the pumpkin-egg mixture until just blended.

orange lemon butter

makes about 350 g/12 oz
225 g/8 oz unsalted butter, softened
Grated rind of 1 orange
1 to 2 tbsp orange juice
Grated rind of 1 lemon

1 tbsp lemon juice
½ tsp vanilla essence
75 g/3 oz caster sugar (or to taste)

Beat all the ingredients together in a medium bowl, using an electric mixer, until light and fluffy. Scrape onto a piece of cling film or greaseproof

3 Divide the mixture equally between the two tins, smoothing the tops evenly. Bake until risen, dark golden and a fine skewer inserted in the centre comes out clean. Remove the tins to a wire rack to cool, about 15 minutes, then turn out, top-side up, onto the wire rack to cool completely. Wrap well and leave to stand overnight for flavours to develop. Serve with Orange Lemon Butter.

paper, and shape into a log. Wrap tightly and refrigerate until firm, about 1 to 2 hours. Slice into rounds and serve.

yeast breads
and
coffee cakes

AUSTRIAN HAZELNUT AND PLUM CAKE

makes 8 servings

*50 g/2 oz whole hazelnuts,
lightly toasted*

75 g/3 oz light brown sugar

70 g/2¾ oz plain flour

*½ tsp freshly grated or
ground nutmeg*

3 egg whites

2 to 3 ripe plums, thinly sliced

⅛ tsp cream of tartar

1 tsp vanilla essence

*40 g/1½ oz unsalted butter,
melted and cooled*

2 tbsp caster sugar

Icing sugar for dusting

Soured cream to serve (optional)

This cake derives from an Austrian-style plum torte. Use a food processor to grind the nuts, but be sure to toast and cool them first as this brings out their flavour.

1 Preheat the oven to 220°C/425°F/gas mark 7. Butter and flour a 20-cm/8-inch spring clip tin. Process the hazelnuts, brown sugar, flour and nutmeg in a food processor fitted with the metal blade, until very finely ground.

2 In a large bowl with an electric mixer, beat the egg whites until frothy. Add the cream of tartar and beat until just stiff. Sprinkle over a tablespoon of white sugar and beat for 30 seconds longer until the whites are stiff and glossy.

3 Sprinkle the nut mixture over the egg whites and fold in gently. Stir the vanilla into the melted butter, then slowly drizzle the butter down the side of the bowl; fold in gently (don't worry if the mixture deflates). Spoon into the prepared tin and smooth the top.

4 Arrange the plum slices in concentric circles over the mixture, then sprinkle with about 2 teaspoons sugar. Bake until puffed and golden, and the cake begins to shrink away from the side of the tin, 20 to 25 minutes. Remove to a wire rack to cool, about 10 minutes. Run a sharp knife between the cake and the side of the tin; unclip and remove the side. Dust the top lightly with icing sugar and serve warm with soured cream, if desired.

BLUEBERRY AND CREAM CHEESE STREUSEL CAKE

makes 10 to 12 servings

streusel topping

115 g/4 oz unsalted butter, softened

175 g/6 oz sugar

50 g/2 oz brown sugar

scant 75 g/3 oz plain flour

50 g/2 oz toasted hazelnuts, chopped

1½ tsp ground cinnamon

½ tsp ground nutmeg

¼ tsp salt

cream cheese filling

350 g/12 oz cream cheese

75 g/3 oz sugar

1 egg

Grated rind of 1 lemon

1 tbsp lemon juice

1 tsp almond essence

cake

450 g/1 lb plain flour

4 tsp baking powder

1 tsp salt

450 g/1 lb unsalted butter

275 g/10 oz sugar

2 eggs, lightly beaten

1 tsp almond essence

275 ml/½ pint milk

450 g/1 lb fresh blueberries

This luscious cake is a cross between a blueberry muffin and a cheesecake—perfect for a brunch, or anytime.

1 Preheat the oven to 190°C/375°F/gas mark 5. Generously butter a 53 x 23-cm/13 x 9-inch glass baking dish. To prepare the topping, rub together all the ingredients with fingertips or a pastry blender in a medium bowl, until well blended and large crumbs form. Set aside.

2 To prepare the filling: soften the cream cheese and beat with the sugar until creamy in a medium bowl using an electric mixer, scraping down the side of the bowl occasionally. Beat in the egg, grated lemon rind and juice and almond essence until smooth. Set aside.

3 To prepare the cake: sift the flour, baking powder and salt into a bowl. In another bowl, with an electric mixer, beat the softened butter and sugar until light and fluffy, about 2 to 3 minutes. Gradually beat in the eggs until very light and smooth. Beat in the almond essence. Beat in the flour mixture on low speed, alternating with the milk and ending with the flour mixture, until well blended. If the mixture is too stiff, add a little more milk. Gently fold in the washed and dried blueberries.

4 Spread slightly less than half the cake mixture on the bottom of the dish, smoothing the surface and pushing into corners. Gently spread the cream cheese filling over the cake mixture, and lightly sprinkle about one quarter of the streusel topping over the filling. Drop spoonfuls of the remaining mixture over the top and spread evenly, trying not to mix the layers. Sprinkle the remaining topping evenly over the surface.

5 Bake until the topping is crunchy and golden brown, and a skewer inserted into the centre comes out with just a few crumbs attached, about 1 hour. Remove to a wire rack and cool until the cake is just warm. Cut into squares and serve slightly warm or at room temperature.

TIP *Be sure to use an ovenproof glass dish, as the blueberries could react with the metal. (A porcelain dish would not allow the cake to cook completely.)*

LEMON AND YOGURT CRUMBLE CAKE

makes 10 to 12 servings

crumble topping

115 g/4 oz sugar

25 g/1 oz plain flour

40 g/1½ oz butter, cut into
small pieces

Grated rind of 1 lemon

cake

225 g/8 oz plain flour

1½ tsp baking powder

½ tsp bicarbonate of soda

¼ tsp salt

25 g/1 oz candied lemon peel,
finely chopped

115 g/4 oz unsalted butter

175 g/6 oz sugar

225 ml/8 fl oz plain yogurt or
buttermilk

2 eggs, lightly beaten

Grated rind of 1 lemon

1 tsp vanilla essence

This moist cake has a rich, lemony flavour, with a crumbly swirl and topping.

1 Preheat the oven to 180°C/350°F/gas mark 4. Grease and lightly flour a 23 x 13-cm/9 x 5-inch loaf tin. Combine the crumble topping ingredients in a small bowl and rub in the butter using your fingertips, until the mixture resembles coarse breadcrumbs; set aside.

2 Sift the flour, baking powder, bicarbonate of soda and salt into a bowl. Stir in the candied lemon peel and make a well in the centre.

3 Put the butter in a saucepan and set over low heat until melted, stirring occasionally. Remove from heat and whisk in the sugar, yogurt, eggs, grated lemon rind, and vanilla essence. Pour into the well and stir with a fork until just blended.

4 Spoon half the mixture into the prepared tin, smoothing the top and pushing into the corners. Sprinkle over half the crumb topping. Drop spoonfuls of the remaining mixture over the topping and spread as evenly as possible, then sprinkle with the remaining topping.

5 Bake until the cake is risen and golden, and a fine skewer inserted in the centre comes out clean, about 1 hour. Remove to a wire rack to cool for at least 30 minutes. Run a thin bladed knife between the cake and the sides of the tin to loosen it, then carefully unmould onto the

rack, top-side up, to cool. This cake is best made a day ahead, wrapped tightly until ready to serve.

LEMONY BRIOCHE LOAF

makes one 23 x 13-cm/
9 x 5-inch loaf **or 12** buns

2 tbsp sugar

3 tbsp water

1 x 7 g/¼ oz packet dried yeast

2 eggs, lightly beaten

115–175 g/4–6 oz plain flour

¾ tsp salt

Grated rind of 1 lemon

75 g/3 oz unsalted butter, cut into
small pieces, softened

1 egg yolk, beaten with
1 tbsp water for glazing

Rich and buttery, classic French brioche is a favourite breakfast treat. It can be baked in a loaf tin, but use the traditional moulds if you like; be sure to start the dough the night before you want the loaf.

1 Put 1 tablespoon of the sugar in a small saucepan with the water, and heat over low heat until very warm (50–55°C/120°F–130°F), stirring to dissolve the sugar. Sprinkle over the yeast and allow to stand until yeast is frothy, about 5 to 10 minutes. Stir to dissolve, then beat in the eggs.

2 Put the flour, salt, grated lemon rind, and remaining sugar in a food processor fitted with a metal blade, and blend. With the machine running, slowly pour the yeast-egg mixture through the feed tube; a dough will form immediately. Scrape down the side of the bowl, and process the dough until very well kneaded, 2 to 3 minutes. Sprinkle over the softened butter pieces and pulse in the butter until just blended, about 12 times.

3 Scrape the dough into a large, greased bowl, turning to grease the top. Cover with a clean teatowel and leave to rise in a warm place (25–30°C/80°F–85°F) until the dough doubles in volume, about 1½ hours. (At this point the dough can be refrigerated overnight to rise very slowly.)

4 Butter a 23 x 13-cm/9 x 5-inch loaf tin. Knock back the dough and turn onto a lightly floured surface; knead lightly 2 to 3 times. Divide the dough into 8 or 9 pieces, and shape into balls. Arrange the dough balls in the tin, pushing them together to fit. Cover and leave to rise in a warm place until just doubled in volume, about 40 minutes.

5 Preheat the oven to 200°C/400°F/gas mark 6. Brush the top of the risen loaf with the egg glaze and bake until well risen and deep golden brown, about 30 minutes. Remove to a wire rack and turn out immediately, top-side up, to cool. Serve warm with butter and jam, if desired.

ALMOND CROISSANTS

makes 24 *croissants*

300 ml/11 fl oz milk

2 tbsp sugar

1 x 7 g/¼ oz packet dried yeast

350–400 g/12–14 oz plain flour

1½ tsp salt

225 g/8 oz unsalted butter

1 egg, with 1 tsp water for glazing

Flaked almonds for sprinkling

Icing sugar for dusting (optional)

almond paste

75 g/3 oz blanched almonds

1 tbsp plain flour

1 tbsp cornflour

115 g/4 oz caster sugar

75 g/3 oz unsalted butter,

cut into pieces, softened

1 egg

1 egg yolk

½ tsp almond essence

TIP *In Step 6, if the butter squeezes out of the packet, or the dough becomes sticky at any time, slide it onto a baking sheet and chill until easier to handle.*

These tender, flaky croissants are filled with a homemade almond paste for an extra luxurious treat. Making them is well worth the effort.

1 In a small saucepan, heat the milk and half of the sugar over low heat until very warm (50–55°C/120°F–130°F). Pour into the bowl of an electric mixer and sprinkle over the yeast and 1 tablespoon of the flour. Allow to stand until frothy, about 15 minutes. With a hand whisk, beat in 115 g/4 oz of the flour, the salt and the remaining sugar.

2 Fit the mixer with the dough hook and gradually beat in 225 g/8 oz of flour on low speed. Beat on high until the dough comes together and begins to pull away from the side of the bowl; if the dough is very wet, sprinkle in a little more flour. Beat until smooth. Scrape the dough into a greased bowl. Cover and leave to rise in a warm place (25–30°C/80°F–85°F) until dough doubles in volume, about 1½ hours.

3 Knock back the dough and turn onto a lightly floured surface; knead lightly until smooth, 4 to 5 times. Wrap in a teatowel and refrigerate about 10 minutes, while preparing the butter.

4 Put the butter between 2 sheets of cling film and roll the butter into a rectangular shape. Fold the butter in half and roll out again. Repeat until butter is smooth and pliable, but still cold. Flatten to form a 15 x 10-cm/6 x 4-inch rectangle.

5 Roll the dough to a 45 x 20-cm/18 x 8-inch rectangle on a lightly floured surface, keeping the centre third thicker than the two outer ends. Put the butter rectangle on the thicker centre of the dough, then fold the bottom third of the dough over the butter. Fold the top third of the dough over the bottom to enclose the butter; with the rolling pin press down the 'open edges' to seal the dough and create a neat dough 'package'.

6 Turn the dough 'package' so that the short 'open edge' faces you, the folded edge is on the left and it resembles a closed book. Gently roll the dough to a rectangle about 45 cm/18 inches long, keeping the edges straight; do not press out the butter. Fold the rectangle in thirds, as for enclosing the butter, and press down the edges to seal. Press your index finger into one corner to mark the first turn clearly. Wrap the dough in cling film and refrigerate for 30 minutes.

7 Repeat the rolling and folding, or 'turns', twice more, wrapping, marking and chilling the dough between each turn. After the third turn, wrap and refrigerate the dough for at least 2 hours.

8 Meanwhile, prepare the almond paste. Put the blanched almonds, flour, cornflour and sugar in the bowl of a food processor and process until

very fine crumbs form. Sprinkle over the butter, the egg, egg yolk and almond essence. Process until a smooth paste forms. If not using immediately, cover and refrigerate.

9 Lightly spray 2 baking sheets. Soften the dough at room temperature, 5 to 10 minutes, for easier rolling. Roll the dough to a 3-mm/⅛-inch thick rectangle about 33 cm/13 inches wide on a lightly floured surface. Trim the edges straight. Cut the rectangle in half to form 2 long strips. Cut each strip into triangles, 15 cm/6 inches high and 10 cm/4 inches wide at the base. Using the rolling pin, roll gently from the base to the point, stretching each triangle lengthways.

10 Place a tablespoon of almond paste about 2.5 cm/1 inch up from the base of each triangle. Pulling the base slightly to widen it, roll up the dough from the base to the point. Arrange point-side down on the baking sheets, curving the ends to form a crescent shape. Brush each croissant with egg glaze; cover and leave to rise in a warm place until almost *tripled* in volume, about 2 hours. (At this point, the formed croissants can be refrigerated overnight and baked the next day.) Refrigerate the egg glaze until ready to bake the croissants.

11 Preheat the oven to 240°C/475°F/gas mark 9. Brush each croissant again with the egg glaze. Sprinkle each with a few flaked almonds. Bake for 2 minutes, then reduce oven temperature to 190°C/375°F/gas mark 5 and bake until golden, about 10 minutes more. Remove to a wire rack and transfer the croissants to the wire rack to cool. Dust lightly with icing sugar and serve.

HONEY WALNUT BREAD

with brown sugar and cream cheese spread

makes 1 loaf

575 ml / 1 pint water

1 tbsp sugar

25 g / 8 oz wholemeal flour

175 g / 6 oz plain flour

2½ tsp salt

2 tbsp honey

water

1 x 7 g / ¼ oz packet dried yeast

115 g / 4 oz walnut halves, chopped, plus extra walnut halves for decoration (optional)

1 egg, lightly beaten for glazing

This dense, nutty, slightly sweet bread is delicious for breakfast, especially with soft cheeses or Brown Sugar and Cream Cheese Spread (see page 12).

1 In a small saucepan over low heat, heat the water and sugar until very warm (50–55°C/ 120°F–130°F). In a large bowl, stir the wholemeal flour, plain flour and salt together until well blended, then make a well in the centre. Stir the honey into warm water and pour into the well. Sprinkle the yeast over it and allow to stand until frothy, about 15 minutes.

2 Pour in the remaining water, then slowly incorporate the flour from the edge of the well into the liquid with an electric mixer on low speed or a wooden spoon, mixing to form a smooth dough. If the dough is very sticky, sprinkle in a little more flour.

3 Turn dough onto a lightly floured surface and knead until smooth and elastic, about 5 minutes. Place the dough in a greased bowl, turning to grease the top. Cover with a clean teatowel or plastic bag and leave to rise in a warm place (25–30°C/80°F–85°F) until doubled in volume, about 1½ hours.

4 Grease a large baking sheet. Knock back the dough and turn onto a lightly floured surface. Sprinkle over the chopped walnuts and knead into the dough until evenly distributed. Shape the dough into a round or oval and place on the baking sheet. Cover with a teatowel and leave in a warm place to rise again until just doubled in volume, about 30 minutes.

5 Preheat the oven to 220°C/425°F/gas mark 7. Brush the loaf with the egg glaze. With a sharp knife, slash the top of the dough in 3 to 4 places and bake for 15 minutes. Reduce the oven temperature to 190°C/375°F/gas mark 5, and bake until the loaf is deep golden brown, about 40 minutes more. Remove to a wire rack, sliding the loaf onto the rack to cool completely. Serve warm with the Brown Sugar and Cream Cheese Spread (see page 12).

STICKY CINNAMON BUNS

with brown sugar and butter topping

makes 18 buns

225 ml/8 fl oz milk

115 g/4 oz butter or margarine

115 g/4 oz sugar

1 tsp salt

1 x 7 g x ¼ oz packet dried yeast

450–500 g/16–18 oz plain flour

2 eggs, lightly beaten

2 tsp vanilla essence

1 tsp ground cinnamon

brown sugar and butter
topping

250 g/9 oz dark brown sugar

75 g/3 oz butter

150 ml/¼ pint water

2 tsp ground cinnamon

75 g/3 oz pecans, chopped

3 tbsp sugar

115 g/4 oz raisins

TIP *To check if the dough has doubled in volume, press a finger into the dough. If the hole remains, the dough is ready to be knocked back.*

These buns are topped with a sugar and butter mixture that caramelises as they bake.

1 Put the milk and butter into a saucepan and heat over low heat until very warm. Meanwhile, stir the sugar, salt, yeast and 115 g/4 oz flour together in a large bowl, then make a well in the centre.

2 Pour the milk into the well and gradually beat with an electric mixer on low speed, until well blended. Beat for 2 minutes. Beat in the eggs, vanilla essence, cinnamon and 115 g/4 oz more of the flour, and continue beating for 2 more minutes. With a wooden spoon, stir in 225 g/ 8 oz flour until a soft dough forms.

3 Turn the dough onto a lightly floured surface, and knead until smooth and elastic, 10 minutes. Shape the dough into a ball and place in a greased bowl, turning to grease the top. Cover with a clean teatowel and leave to rise in a warm place (25–30°C/80°F–85°F), about 2 hours.

4 Meanwhile, prepare the topping. Put the brown sugar, butter, water and half the cinnamon in a saucepan, and heat over low heat until the sugar dissolves and the butter is melted. Bring to the boil and simmer until syrupy, about 8 minutes. Pour about 1 tablespoon of the syrup into the bottom of an 18-cup muffin tin. Sprinkle in a little of the chopped pecans, sugar and raisins into each cup.

5 Knock back the dough and place on a lightly floured surface, then roll into a rectangle, about 45 x 30 cm/18 x 12 inches. Sprinkle evenly with the remaining pecans, sugar, raisins and cinnamon. Beginning with a long side, roll the dough Swiss-roll style to form a log. With a sharp knife, cut into eighteen 2.5-cm/1-inch slices, and place each slice in a prepared muffin cup, cut-side up. Cover and leave to rise, about 45 minutes.

6 Preheat the oven to 190°C/375°F/gas mark 5. Bake until risen and well coloured, about 25 minutes. Remove muffins from the oven and invert onto a Swiss-roll tin; *do not remove* the muffin tins, but allow each to cool for 3 minutes. Remove the muffin tins. Transfer the buns to the rack to cool; serve warm, sticky-side up.

SPICY SWEET POTATO BREAD

makes 12 to 14 servings

225 ml/8 fl oz water

275 g/10 oz sugar

2 x 7g/¼ oz packets dried yeast

625 g/1 lb 6 oz plain flour

1 tsp salt

4 tsp pumpkin-pie or mixed spice

50 g/2 oz instant, nonfat dry milk

225 g/8 oz sweet potato or

pumpkin, mashed, cooked or

canned

115 g/4 oz butter, melted and

cooled

Grated rind of 1 orange

50 g/2 oz walnuts or pecans,

chopped

This mellow, well-coloured bread is like a sweet potato pie—warm and spicy. It is perfect for a winter brunch or coffee morning.

1 In a small saucepan over low heat, heat the water and 1 tablespoon of the sugar until very warm (50–55°C/120°F–130°F). Pour into the bowl of a heavy-duty electric mixer and sprinkle over the yeast and 1 tablespoon of the flour. Allow to stand until frothy, about 15 minutes.

2 Fit the mixer with the dough hook and beat in the salt, 2 teaspoons of the spice, the dry milk, mashed sweet potato or pumpkin, 115 g/4 oz of the sugar, half the butter, the grated orange rind and 225 g/8 oz of the flour until well blended.

3 On low speed, gradually beat in the remaining flour; continue to beat on medium speed until a rough dough forms. Turn the dough onto a lightly floured surface and knead until smooth, 10 to 12 times. Place the dough in a greased bowl, turning to grease the top. Cover with a clean teatowel and leave to rise in a warm place (25–30°C/80°F –85°F) until doubled in volume, 1 to 1½ hours.

4 Knock back the dough and turn onto a lightly floured surface; knead 2 to 3 times. Cut the dough into 3 equal pieces, then roll each into a cylinder about 45 cm/18 inches long. Cut each cylinder into 18 pieces, then roll each piece into a ball.

5 Generously grease a 25-cm/10-inch tube tin. Combine the remaining sugar and spice in a small bowl. Roll the dough balls in the remaining butter and then into the sugar mixture. Arrange the balls in the bottom of the prepared tin, and sprinkle over half of the chopped nuts. Arrange the remaining balls over the first layer, pushing into the creases and pressing together to fit. Sprinkle over the remaining nuts. Cover with the teatowel and leave in a warm place until just doubled, about 45 minutes.

5 Preheat the oven to 180°C/350°F/gas mark 4. Bake until risen and well coloured, about 1 hour. Remove to a wire rack to cool, for 10 to 15 minutes, then turn out onto the wire rack to cool, top-side up, until just warm. Serve with a flavoured butter, if you like.

SUNNY RAISIN BREAD

makes 2 loaves

100 ml/4 fl oz water

scant 75 g/3 oz sugar

1 x 7 g/¼ oz packet dried yeast

175 g/6 oz raisins

75 g/3 oz sultanas

Grated rind of 1 orange and

juice of ½ orange

½ tsp freshly grated nutmeg

325 ml/12 fl oz milk

1 tbsp salt

1 tsp ground cinnamon

115 g/4 oz butter, melted

575–675 g/1¼–1½ lb plain flour

1 egg, beaten with 1 tbsp milk

for glazing

Toasted raisin bread is a special, childhood weekend treat in many houses. Some prefer it toasted and buttered, and sprinkled with a mixture of sugar and ground cinnamon.

1 Heat the water and 1 tablespoon of the sugar in a small saucepan over low heat, until very warm (50–55°C/120°F–130°F). Pour into the bowl of a heavy-duty electric mixer and sprinkle over the yeast. Allow to stand until frothy, about 15 minutes. Meanwhile, lightly mix the raisins and sultanas in a medium bowl with the grated orange rind, juice and grated nutmeg, then set aside.

2 Whisk the milk, remaining sugar, salt, cinnamon, half the butter and 115 g/4 oz of the flour into the yeast mixture until blended. Fit the mixer with the dough hook and beat in 225–350 g/8–12 oz of flour on low speed until a dough forms. Gradually beat in the remaining flour until a firm dough forms; you may not need all the flour.

3 Turn the dough onto a lightly floured surface and knead until smooth and elastic, about 5 minutes. Place the dough in a greased bowl, turning to grease the top. Cover with a clean teatowel and leave to rise in a warm place (25–30°C/80°F–85°F) until doubled in volume, about 2 hours.

4 Knock back the dough and knead 2 to 3 times. Return to the bowl, cover and leave to rise in a warm place for 30 minutes more.

5 Grease two 20 x 10 cm/8 x 4-inch loaf tins. Place the dough on a lightly floured surface and cut in half. With a lightly floured rolling pin, roll each half into a rectangle about 45 x 20-cm/18 x 8 inches. Brush the rectangles with the remaining butter, then sprinkle half the raisin mixture over each. Beginning at a short end, roll the dough tightly, Swiss-roll style. Place in the tins, tucking the ends down and under. Cover and leave in a warm place to rise again, until just doubled in volume.

6 Preheat the oven to 200°C/400°F/gas mark 6. Brush the top of each loaf with the egg glaze and bake for 20 minutes. Reduce the oven temperature to 180°C/350°F/gas mark 4, and bake until golden brown, about 25 minutes more. Remove the loaves to a wire rack and turn out immediately, top-side up, to cool. If you like, serve with Orange Lemon Butter (see page 58).

CHOCOLATE POPPY SEED PLAIT

makes 12 to 14 servings

4 tbsp water

50 g/2 oz sugar

1 x 7 g/¼ oz packet dried yeast

4 tbsp lukewarm milk

½ tsp salt

1 egg, lightly beaten

50 g/2 oz butter, softened

350–400 g/12–14 oz plain flour

1 egg yolk, beaten with 1 tbsp milk

for glazing

chocolate poppy seed filling

115 g/4 oz poppy seeds

50 g/2 oz sugar

40 g/1½ oz raisins

½ tsp ground cinnamon

Grated rind of ½ orange

4 tbsp soured cream

1 tbsp marmalade or apricot jam

75 g/3 oz plain chocolate chips

This sweet yeast dough is filled with a rich, poppy seed and chocolate chip mixture before being plaited. It makes a beautiful addition to any breakfast or brunch table.

1 In a small saucepan over low heat, heat the water and 1 tablespoon sugar until very warm (50–55°C/120°F–130°F). Pour into the bowl of a heavy-duty electric mixer, and sprinkle over the yeast. Allow to stand until frothy, about 15 minutes.

2 Fit the mixer with the dough hook and beat in the warm milk, remaining sugar, salt, egg, and butter. On low speed, gradually beat in 350 g/ 12 oz of the flour until a soft dough forms. If the dough is sticky, add a little more flour. Beat until the dough comes together and becomes elastic.

3 Turn the dough onto a lightly floured surface, and knead until smooth and elastic, 2 to 3 minutes, adding a little more flour if necessary. Place the dough in a greased bowl, turning to grease the top. Cover with a clean teatowel and leave to rise in a warm place (25–30°C/80°F– 85°F) until doubled in volume, about 1½ hours.

4 Meanwhile, prepare the filling. Put all the ingredients, except the chocolate chips, in the bowl of a food processor fitted with the metal blade. Process, using the pulse button, until just well blended but not completely smooth. Grease a large baking sheet.

5 Knock back the dough and turn onto a lightly floured surface, kneading 2 to 3 times. With a lightly floured rolling pin, roll into a rectangle about 38 x 25 cm/15 x 10 inches. To transfer to the baking sheet, roll the dough around the rolling pin and carefully unroll onto the baking sheet, stretching gently to keep the shape. Spread the filling down the centre third of the dough, to within about 5 cm/2 inches from each end.

6 With a sharp knife, cut 8 to 10 diagonal slashes from both sides of the filling to both edges of the dough, cutting about 1 cm/½ inch from the filling. Beginning at one end, fold the end over the bottom edge of the filling, then fold over all the strips from alternate sides. Tuck the ends of the strips under the plait. Cover with the teatowel and leave in a warm place to rise again until almost doubled in volume.

7 Preheat the oven to 190°C/375°F/gas mark 5. Brush the plait with the egg glaze, then bake until golden and well browned, about 30 minutes. Remove the baking sheet to a wire rack to cool, 15 to 20 minutes, then carefully transfer the plait onto the rack to cool until just warm.

PANETTONE

makes 1 loaf

150 ml/¼ pint milk, plus extra for
glazing

scant 75 g/3 oz sugar

1 x 7 g/¼ oz packet dried yeast

350–400 g/12–14 oz plain flour

2 eggs

5 egg yolks

1 tsp almond essence

Grated rind of 1 lemon

2 tsp salt

175 g/6 oz unsalted butter,
softened

75 g/3 oz raisins

40 g/1½ oz sultanas

50 g/2 oz chopped, candied citrus
peel

25 g/1 oz toasted natural
almonds, chopped

2 tbsp flaked almonds

Sugar for sprinkling

This popular Italian cake is studded with raisins and candied fruit, and is perfect with an espresso coffee or café latte. There is no need to buy a special baking tin to achieve its classic, cylindrical shape; use a charlotte mould to get the same effect.

1 In a small saucepan over low heat, heat the milk and 1 tablespoon of the sugar until very warm (50–55°C/120°F–130°F). Pour into a large mixing bowl, and sprinkle over the yeast. Allow to stand until frothy, about 15 minutes.

2 Sift 115 g/4 oz of the flour over the yeast mixture and with a wooden spoon, stir until a batter forms. Cover the bowl with a clean teatowel and leave in a warm place (25–30°C/ 80°F–85°F) until mixture looks puffy and spongy, about 30 minutes.

3 Whisk the eggs and egg yolks together with the almond essence, grated lemon rind and salt in another bowl. Sift another 225 g/8 oz of flour over the risen yeast flour mixture and make a well in the centre. Pour in the egg mixture and stir with a wooden spoon until the mixture becomes a soft, sticky dough; the dough should be as soft as possible, so do not add more flour unless it is very wet.

4 Using your hand, spread the butter over the dough and work into the dough, folding it over itself and kneading into the dough until the butter is completely incorporated. Cover with

the teatowel and leave to rise again in a warm place until doubled in volume, about 3 hours.

5 Butter a 1.75-litre/3-pint charlotte mould. Line the bottom with nonstick baking parchment and butter again. Knock back the dough and turn onto a lightly floured surface. Sprinkle the raisins, sultanas, citrus peel and almonds over the dough, and knead until evenly distributed throughout the dough.

6 Form the dough into a ball shape and ease into the mould. Cover and leave to rise again until the dough reaches the top of the mould, about 1½ hours.

7 Preheat the oven to 200°C/400°F/gas mark 6. Brush the top of the dough with a little milk and if you like sprinkle with the almonds and about a tablespoon of sugar. Bake for 15 minutes, then reduce the oven temperature to 180°C/350°F/gas mark 4 and bake about 30 minutes longer; if the cake browns too quickly, cover with foil. Remove to a wire rack to cool in the mould for about 5 minutes, then carefully turn out, top-side up, to cool completely.

APRICOT-FILLED DANISH RING

makes 10 to 12 servings

100 ml/4 fl oz water

50 g/2 oz sugar

1 x 7 g/¼ oz packet dried yeast

275 g/10 oz plain flour

1 tsp salt

1 egg, lightly beaten

½ tsp vanilla essence

½ tsp almond essence

225 g/8 oz unsalted butter

1 egg yolk, beaten with

1 tbsp water, for glazing

Flaked almonds for sprinkling

apricot filling

175 g/16 oz dried 'no-soak'

apricots

25 g/1 oz butter, softened

2 tbsp honey or sugar to taste

Grated rind of 1 lemon plus

1 tbsp lemon juice

½ tsp almond essence

1 to 2 tbsp apricot jam

glaze

50 g/2 oz icing sugar

2 to 3 tbsp lemon juice or water

This luxurious Danish bake is filled with a purée of dried apricots and drizzled with a sugar glaze—a classic for coffee mornings or any occasion.

1 In a saucepan over low heat, heat the water and 1 tablespoon sugar until very warm (50–55°C/120°F–130°F). Pour into a bowl and sprinkle over the yeast; allow to stand until frothy, about 15 minutes. Stir the flour, remaining sugar and salt to blend, and make a well in the centre.

2 Whisk the egg, vanilla and almond essences into the yeast mixture and pour into the well. Stir with a wooden spoon until a rough dough forms. Place on a lightly floured surface and knead until smooth and elastic, about 5 minutes. Wrap in cling film and refrigerate for about 10 minutes while preparing the butter.

3 Put the butter between 2 sheets of cling film and with a rolling pin, roll into a rectangular shape. Fold the butter in half and roll out again. Repeat until butter is pliable, but still cold. Flatten to form a 15 x 10-cm/6 x 4-inch rectangle.

4 On a lightly floured surface, with a lightly floured rolling pin, roll the dough to a 45 x 20-cm/18 x 8-inch rectangle, keeping the centre third thicker than the two outer ends. Put the butter rectangle on the thicker centre of the dough and fold the bottom third of the dough over the butter. Fold the top third of the dough over the bottom to enclose the butter; with the rolling pin, press down the 'open edges' to seal the dough to create a neat dough 'package'.

5 Turn the dough 'package' so that the short 'open edge' faces you and the folded edge is on the left and package resembles a closed book. Gently roll the dough to a rectangle about 45 cm/18 inches long, keeping the edges straight; do not press out the butter. Fold the rectangle in thirds, as for enclosing the butter and press down the edges to seal. Press a finger into one corner to clearly mark the first turn. Wrap the dough tightly in cling film or the teatowel and refrigerate for 30 minutes.

6 Repeat the rolling and folding, or turns, twice more, wrapping, marking and chilling the dough between each turn. After the third turn, wrap and refrigerate the dough for at least 2 hours.

7 Meanwhile prepare the filling. Put all the filling ingredients in the bowl of a food processor and process until smooth; set aside. Grease a large baking sheet.

8 Soften the dough at room temperature, 5 to 10 minutes, for easier rolling. On a lightly floured surface, roll the dough to a rectangle of about 70 x 30 cm/28 x 12 inches. Spread the apricot filling to within 2.5 cm/1 inch of the edges.

Beginning at one long side, fold or roll the dough loosely, about 3 times, Swiss-roll style. Transfer to the baking sheet and bring the two ends together. Brush one end with a little water and pinch the edges together to seal, forming a ring.

9 Using floured kitchen scissors held perpendicular to the ring, make diagonal snips, 4 cm/1½ inches apart, into the outer edge of the ring, to within 2.5 cm/1 inch of the inner edge. Gently pull and twist every other slice of the ring towards the outer edge. Pull and twist the alternating slices toward the centre to expose the spiral effect of the filling. Cover with a clean teatowel and leave in a warm place to rise again until just doubled, about 40 minutes.

10 Preheat the oven to 200°C/400°F/gas mark 6. Brush with the egg glaze and sprinkle with flaked almonds. Bake until golden, about 35 minutes; cover with foil if the ring browns too quickly. Remove to a wire rack to cool, about 10 minutes, then slide onto the wire rack, top-side up, to cool. While the ring is still warm, stir the icing sugar and lemon juice or water together until smooth, then drizzle over the ring.